The Garlic Lovers' Cookbook

©1979 G.G.F.A., Inc.

From Gilroy, California

Garlic Capital of the World

Celestial Arts
Berkeley • Toronto

Celestial Arts Publishing
P.O. Box 7123
Berkeley, California 94707
www.tenspeed.com

Celestial Arts titles are distributed in Canada by Ten Speed Canada, in the United Kingdom and Europe by Airlift Books, in South Africa by Real Books, in Australia by Simon & Schuster Australia, and in New Zealand by Southern Publishers Group.

Cover design by Toni Tajima
Front Cover photography by Chad Slattery/ Stone/ Getty Images
Back Cover photography by Bill Strange
Text design by Jeff Brandenburg/image-comp.com

Library of Congress Cataloging in Publication Data

Gilroy Garlic Festival Committee.
     The garlic lovers cookbook.
     Includes index.
     1. Cookery (Garlic)   1. Title.
TX819.G3G54   1980   641.6526   80-66298

ISBN 1-58761-129-5

Printed in the United States of America
1 2 3 4 5 6 7 / 09 08 07 06 05 04 03

Dedication

Garlic lovers everywhere have much in common: the joy of eating and cooking with this marvelous seasoning, of course, and an appreciation of the wonderful lore that surrounds garlic, both historical and medicinal. But even more than this, we share in the aura of garlic. We respond to this simple bulb's invitation to enjoy life's pleasures—to appreciate great food, close friends, and good times together.

In this spirit of conviviality, we have lovingly compiled this cookbook from time-tested and cherished recipes of local residents, professional and amateur chefs in the area, from entries in Gilroy's annual Great Garlic Cook-off Recipe Contest, and from Gilroy's own fresh garlic growers, shippers, and processors.

This book is dedicated in friendship by the citizens of Gilroy to garlic lovers the world over. We also extend a personal invitation to each of you to visit us during the last full weekend of July each year for our Garlic Festival. Join us in paying tribute to garlic... and to Gilroy, Garlic Capital of the World!

Acknowledgments

The Gilroy Garlic Festival Association gratefully acknowledges the participation of the many garlic lovers whose Herculean efforts have produced this unique cookbook.

For their contributions and support, our appreciation and thanks to:

· Garlic Lovers' Cookbook Committee Members: Betty Angelino, Karen Christopher, Fred Domino, Tim Filice, Nori Goforth, Mary Mozzone, Rose Emma Pelliccione, Dale Springer

· A&D Christopher Ranch

· Caryl Saunders Associates

· Fresh Garlic Association

· Foremost Gentry International

· Gilroy Foods, Inc.

· Miller, Perrin, Domino, Giacalone & Ackerman, Attorneys at Law

A special thanks to the generous donors of the courtesy recipes, the recipe contest participants, and the unheralded, behind-the-scenes recipe testers (and their families) who tasted and critiqued hundreds of garlic recipes.

We invite each of you garlic fanciers with a special recipe to participate in the next annual Great Garlic Cook-off Recipe Contest, held during the Gilroy Garlic Festival each year at the end of July. Contest details are available at the Festival's web site (www.gilroygarlicfestival.com) or by calling the office at 408-842-1625.

As one enthusiastic food editor wrote, "The time has come for garlic to come storming out of the pantry closet." We're doing our best...

Here's to more garlic in our lives!

Gilroy Garlic Festival Association, Inc.
P.O. Box 2311
Gilroy, California 95021
408-842-1625
www.gilroygarlicfestival.com

Contents

The Gilroy Garlic Festival

In 1979, most people had never heard of Gilroy, California. Garlic was still a somewhat exotic herb used mostly in Italian and Asian cuisines. Even some residents of Gilroy had no idea their small town had a legitimate claim as the "garlic capital of the world."

Dr. Rudy Melone, who had recently moved to Gilroy, proposed hosting an annual festival to celebrate the end of the garlic harvest and raise money for local charities. Garlic grower/shipper Don Christopher and chef Val Filice thought it was a crazy idea, but they (along with hundreds of other volunteers) agreed to help. The rest is history. An anticipated first-year attendance of 5,000 jumped to 15,000, and the city of Gilroy and its now-famous Garlic Festival have continued to grow ever since, drawing crowds of 125,000 or more each year at the end of July.

Though much has changed since 1979, Gilroy's community spirit and love (and aroma) of garlic remain just as strong as ever. The Garlic Festival is now powered by more than 4,000 community volunteers, doing everything imaginable, from selling tickets and parking cars to chopping vegetables, serving food, and pouring wine. Their hard work and dedication have made the

Garlic Festival one of the premier food festivals in the world. And, along the way, these volunteers have raised almost $6 million for local schools, charities, service clubs, and nonprofit organizations.

Guests arriving at Christmas Hill park, the Festival's site since 1980, can find ongoing musical entertainment on three stages, including rock, country, jazz, bluegrass, reggae, swing, and much more. Younger visitors enjoy many different hands-on art activities, games, and live entertainment in the shady Children's Area. Each year there are different attractions for older kids (and kids-at-heart); past Festivals have featured rock-climbing walls, extreme sports demonstrations, water gun wars, and giant inflatable slides. Garlic braid and garlic-topping demonstrations are always popular. And Mr. Garlic, dressed in a custom-designed bulb, roams the grounds throughout the Festival, as does the Garlic Queen and her court.

The Garlic Festival's Arts & Crafts areas showcase over one hundred fine artists and craftspeople who offer a wide variety of unique, handmade creations, including paintings, photographs, jewelry, clothing, ceramics, and furniture. And the Garlic Mercantile boutiques feature clothing, cookbooks (including this one!), wine glasses, art posters, and many other garlic-themed gifts and Festival souvenirs.

A special event at each Festival is the Great Garlic Recipe Contest and Cook-off. Entrants from across the nation compete to be among the finalists who get to come to Gilroy and prepare their favorite garlic dishes. The winner is chosen by a panel of illustrious judges, including prominent food writers and professional chefs. Some of the winning recipes from past contests are included in this cookbook.

At the center of the Festival is Gourmet Alley, the giant open-air kitchen where, for love and charity, hundreds of talented townspeople prepare culinary delights until the air is redolent with the fragrance of garlic. Festival-goers can watch the Pyro Chefs cook up garlic-laced calamari and scampi in huge iron skillets. An army of volunteers help prepare other favorites, such as pasta con pesto, marinated pepper steak sandwiches, stuffed mushrooms, sausage sandwiches, and, of course, huge slabs of garlic bread. Other food booths throughout the grounds offer still more garlicky delights, including garlic olives, escargot, pot stickers, pistachios, egg rolls, kettle corn, pickles, catfish, crawdads, pizza, and garlic fries—even rattlesnake and frog legs! And, finally, visitors seeking the full Garlic Festival experience cannot leave without tasting the infamous only-in-Gilroy garlic ice cream. Rest assured, this recipe is *not* included here!

Many of the favorites contained in these pages have been around much longer than the Gilroy Garlic Festival. But it is the Festival that has provided an international showcase for the talents of the townspeople of Gilroy. And it is the Festival that has made this cookbook a possibility and enabled its editors to wrest so many cherished recipes from the chefs of Gilroy. For that we are grateful.

Garlic History and Mystery

Throughout history, as today, garlic was either revered or reviled, depending upon personal tastes and the dictates of society. One of the oldest of cultivated plants and a member of the lily family, along with onions, chives, shallots, and leeks, it was known in Olde English as *garleac*. Its scientific name is *Allium sativum*, which has given rise to the term "alliumphiles" or garlic lovers—those for whom this cookbook will hold particular allure.

The garlic plant has flat, grayish green leaves which grow to be one or two feet tall, but the part of the plant revered in song and story and treasured over the centuries is the bulb. Mentioned over 5000 years ago in Sanskrit, the first written language, garlic was a staple in the ancient Sumerian diet. According to the Greek historian, Herodotus, Egyptian workers who built the Pyramid of Cheops refused to work without their daily portion of garlic. Garlic was even found entombed with King Tutankhamun.

Garlic is known to have been planted in the gardens of the King of Babylon and Homer praised it for its health-giving properties. Roman soldiers and gladiators girded themselves for battle with doses of garlic from which they expected to derive both strength and courage. The Romans also considered it an aphrodisiac, which is why, some historians suggest, they ate so much of it.

Thought to have originated in Siberia, garlic and its culture spread widely, and Marco Polo, mentioned its many uses in his journals. Crusaders returning from their battles in the Holy Land are credited with introducing garlic to northern Europe, where at one time it was so popular that banquet guests were requested to compose verses saluting it. In Boccaccio's *The Decameron*, a love-stricken young man sent garlic to his lady in order to win her love—and he succeeded!

The Magic of Garlic

Undoubtedly because of its potent scent and flavor, in ancient times garlic was thought to have mystical properties and was used as a defense against both known and unknown forces of evil. Even today there are those who hang wreaths of garlic to protect their homes or single cloves about their necks to guard against sinister spirits, and in some cultures it is still considered a sign of great good fortune to dream about garlic. The custom in Balkan countries was to rub garlic on doorknobs and window frames to discourage vampires.

But legend is not all on the positive side. A Mohammedan folktale explains that when Satan was ejected from the Garden of Eden, garlic sprang up wherever he set down his feet, and in 1330 King Alfonso XI of Castile is said to have founded a knightly order based entirely on hatred of garlic.

Medicinal Folklore

But what about garlic's curative powers? In antiquity, a common name for garlic was "cure-all." Over the centuries this simple bulb has steadfastly maintained its reputation for healing everything from infections to high blood pressure to tuberculosis.

The ancient Greeks and Romans prescribed garlic for hundreds of specific ailments. On the other hand, 16th-century Parisians were promised good health the year 'round if they would but eat garlic with fresh butter during the month of May. The British used garlic to control infection during World War I, and in Russia it was used to control rampaging flu epidemics.

Truly there is more lore surrounding the tiny clove of garlic than around any other food. Folk traditions from many cultures say that a cold will surely be cured if one rubs the soles of the feet with cut cloves of garlic. For toothache, there are two schools of thought: one, that a sliver of garlic placed in the cavity of the tooth will relieve the ache; the other, that the sufferer should place a slice of garlic in the ear. For earache, a cut clove should be rubbed over and around the ear.

History records that King Henry V was anointed at birth with wine and garlic because it was believed that garlic on a baby's lips served as a stimulant and an antiseptic. One might argue here more in favor of the wine. But Millin, writing in 1792, praised garlic as a preventive remedy against the plague, and Bernardin de Saint-Pierre recorded that garlic cured nervous maladies.

Scientific proof or no, the belief that garlic can "cure what ails you" persists to this day. But whether or not medical science ever reaches any definite conclusions about the curative powers of garlic seems of little consequence to true garlic lovers. Most important is the magic which garlic performs in the kitchen. The delicious flavors that result from blending garlic with other foods can only be described as pure witchcraft.

Good Things to Know About Garlic

Like most important foods, there are certain basic things to know about garlic. The following information has been assembled to help you identify the various forms of garlic found on the market and make better use of them in your cooking.

Selection and Storage

Fresh garlic, which may be creamy white or have a purplish-red cast, should be plump and firm, with its paper-like covering intact—not spongy, soft, or shriveled. Store in a cool, dry place with adequate ventilation. Refrigeration is not recommended. However, if fresh garlic must be kept for a long time, it can be peeled and the whole cloves dropped into olive oil and stored in the refrigerator for as long as 3 months. Garlic which is held in open-air storage for any length of time will lose much of its pungency. If it does, or if sprouts develop, the garlic is still usable, but it will be somewhat milder, and more may be needed to achieve the same strength of flavor in the dish being prepared.

Dehydrated forms of garlic should be purchased in lightly sealed containers, preferably from markets where there is sufficient turnover to ensure that the spices are fresh. Store in as cool and dry a place as possible, definitely not above or next to the kitchen range, sink, or in front of a window with exposure to the sun. Keep tightly sealed.

Peeling and Cooking Techniques

Peeling garlic can be a problem. One way is to press each clove against the cutting board with the flat side of a heavy kitchen knife. Or pour hot water over the cloves for just a few seconds. This will loosen the skin and allow it to be pulled off easily with a paring knife. The cloves may also be soaked in cool water for about a half-hour before peeling. Or place in a microwave oven for 5 seconds or so.

When cooking garlic in hot oil, remember that it burns easily and when burned, the flavor is not as palatable. When garlic is cooked for a long time, it becomes very mellow and nut-like in flavor and can be spread on bread and potatoes like butter.

Garlic flavors foods differently, depending on how it is used. It is most pungent when eaten raw, especially crushed or minced. Whole cloves or large pieces will give off a gentler flavor.

Each clove of fresh garlic contains only one or two calories. It is especially good as a flavoring in low-sodium diets and is unusually good in dishes which contain onions.

Odor

Fresh parsley, or other foods high in chlorophyll content, will help prevent garlic odor on the breath. Parsley has been called "nature's mouthwash."

To remove the odor of garlic from the hands, rub with salt or lemon juice and then rinse under cold water. Repeat if necessary. If the odor of garlic or onions has permeated a plastic bowl or storage container, wash thoroughly, then crumple a piece of newspaper, add to the container, and cover tightly. The odor should disappear within a few days.

Fresh/Dehydrated Garlic Equivalents

Fresh and dehydrated garlic may be used interchangeably. We offer the following equivalents for converting recipes:

· 1 average size clove fresh garlic = ¼ teaspoon dehydrated powdered, minced, or chopped garlic

· 1 average size clove fresh garlic = ½ teaspoon garlic salt. (Caution: when using garlic salt in recipes calling for fresh garlic, decrease the amount of salt called for.)

Recommended Use Proportions

For the beginner, we offer the following proportions of fresh or dehydrated garlic. Keep in mind that these are on the low side and most who really enjoy the flavor of garlic will want to use a great deal more.

Meats: For each 2 pounds of pork, beef, lamb, or other meats, use ⅛ to ¼ teaspoon garlic powder, or 1½ to 2 teaspoons garlic salt, or 2 or 3 cloves fresh garlic.

Sauces: For 3 cups barbecue, tomato, or other sauce, use ⅛ to ¼ teaspoon garlic powder or 2 or 3 cloves fresh garlic.

Soups: To 3 cups meat stock or vegetable soup, add ⅛ teaspoon garlic powder, or 2 cloves fresh garlic.

Pickled foods: Per 1 quart of kosher-style dill pickles or per 1 pint of dilled green beans, add ⅛ to ¼ teaspoon dehydrated chopped or minced garlic or 2 to 3 cloves fresh garlic.

Relishes: To 2 pints of chutney or relish, add ⅛ teaspoon dehydrated minced garlic, or 2 cloves fresh garlic.

Appetizers/Antipasti

In medieval times, garlic was considered to be a remedy for loss of appetite. In the twenty-first century, garlic is still revered for the same attribute. Consider the delectable morsels we serve to start the meal with a burst of flavor that whet the appetite and provide inspiration and anticipation.

Quick and Easy Appetizers

For an easy cheese spread, combine cream cheese, grated sharp cheese, seasoned salt, and minced garlic with enough mayonnaise to moisten. Shape into a ball or log and roll in chopped nuts. Serve with crackers.

You can make aioli—the French garlic mayonnaise—in a hurry. To 1 cup of ordinary mayonnaise, add 2 or 3 finely chopped fresh garlic cloves. Serve as a dip for vegetables or as a sauce for meats or fish.

Stuff ripe or green pitted olives with almonds. Place stuffed olives in a jar with liquid from kosher or spicy pickles and 5 or 6 cloves of fresh garlic. Chill for 24 hours.

Spinach dip is lovely with crackers or vegetable sticks. Cook a package of frozen spinach, squeezing out the water. Add chopped green onions, minced parsley, 2 cloves of minced garlic, and enough mayonnaise to make a thick dip consistency. Add salt to taste.

Peel fresh garlic cloves and sauté in a small amount of oil sprinkled with oregano. Turn often until well browned. Drain on paper towels and sprinkle with coarsely ground salt. Serve warm for nibbling with cold beverages.

"Smell that!" Mike Filice commanded, and then thrust his own nose into his 30-clove garlic sauce. "Heaven on earth!"

Elizabeth Mahren, *Oakland Tribune*

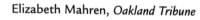

Antipasto Aglio

This wonderful and imaginative appetizer is the creation of one of Gilroy's finest amateur chefs who devised it for his companions on a hunting trip. When prepared this way, the garlic's assertive flavor is diminished to a delicate, nut-like taste. This recipe was selected as a finalist in the First Great Garlic Recipe Contest.

Recipe contest finalist: M. J. Filice, Gilroy

30 large cloves fresh garlic
1 (2-oz.) can of anchovies
1 tbsp. butter, melted
1 tbsp. olive oil
Dash of Tabasco
¼ cup olive oil
1 baguette, thinly sliced and toasted

PREPARATION:
Peel garlic cloves and slice centers ⅛ inch thick. Pass ends through a garlic press to yield ¼ tsp. Place pressed garlic in a small bowl with anchovies. Add parsley, butter, 1 tsp. oil, and Tabasco; mash to a paste. Cover and refrigerate. Heat ¼ cup oil, add garlic slices, and sauté to a light golden brown—*almost* to a potato chip fry. Do not over fry! Spread anchovy paste on toast. Garnish with garlic slices and WHAM-O!—the taste of tastes! Follow with a sip of robust red wine. Salute e buon appetito!

Makes about ½ cup

Dave's Favorite Garlic Dip

Everyone likes garlic dip, and sometimes the simpler it is the better it is. Serve with chips or crackers or use to stuff celery. Great!

Recipe contest entry: Lois Biggs, Gilroy

---

1 (8-oz.) package cream cheese
3 tbsp. milk
5 large cloves fresh garlic
Salt
Parsley
Paprika

PREPARATION:
With a fork, mix cream cheese and milk in a small bowl until it has the texture of peanut butter. Press garlic and add to cream cheese mixture. Salt to taste. Garnish with parsley and paprika. Refrigerate until ready to serve.

Makes about 1 cup

Garlic Guacamole

This is no ordinary guacamole! It's a uniquely aromatic variation. Once you start eating it you won't stop until you've scraped the bowl clean.

Recipe contest entry: Chris Ursich, San Mateo

---

1 ripe avocado
¼ lb. tofu, firm-style
4 to 6 cloves fresh garlic
½ medium bell pepper, finely chopped
2 green onions, minced
2 tbsp. fresh parsley, chopped
½ tsp. curry powder
½ tsp. oregano
½ tsp. thyme
½ tsp. freshly ground black pepper
4 to 6 tbsp. hot sauce
Juice of ½ lime (or lemon)
Tortilla chips for dipping

PREPARATION:
Mash avocado and tofu together in a bowl. Squeeze garlic through press and add. Add bell pepper and green onion and stir to combine. Add herbs and spices. Mix well. Add hot sauce. Stir in lime juice. Serve with tortilla chips. Garlic Guacamole can be refrigerated, but make it no more than a few hours in advance of serving.

Makes about 1 cup

Eggplant Dip Solano

Everyone who has tried this says it's great for a company dish, and inexpensive as well.

Recipe contest entry: Ruth Solano, San Jose

1 eggplant
¼ onion, minced
3 cloves fresh garlic, minced or pressed
Olive oil
Salt and pepper to taste

PREPARATION:
Cook eggplant in heavy skillet over low heat, turning frequently until skin is dark and crackles to the touch. Cool, peel, then mash pulp; add onion and garlic. Add oil, a little at a time, while continuing to mash, until mixture is creamy in texture. Eggplant absorbs oil, so quite a bit is needed. Add salt and pepper. Refrigerate. May be used as a dip for vegetables or on chunks of pita bread as a spread.

Makes 1½ to 2 cups

"Too Easy" Garlic Spread

A tasty spread that's easy to put together in a hurry when friends or family arrive unexpectedly. If you don't have French bread, serve with your favorite crackers.

Courtesy of: Doris Lane, Gilroy

---

2 cups grated Cheddar cheese
¼ cup (approx.) mayonnaise
1 cloves fresh garlic, minced
1 tsp. dehydrated parsley flakes
French bread, sliced

PREPARATION:
Combine grated cheese, mayonnaise, and garlic. Mix well. Be sure it is moist, increasing mayonnaise if necessary. Refrigerate for 1 or 2 hours to allow flavors to mingle. Preheat broiler. When ready to serve, spread mixture on muffins or French bread and broil until cheese is melted. Garnish with parsley.

Makes about 2 cups

Bagno Caldo

The name of this sauce, a specialty of the Piedmont region of Italy, literally means "hot bath." Keep it hot by serving from a chafing dish.

6 large cloves fresh garlic
1 cup sweet butter
¼ cup olive oil
2 tbsp. chopped anchovies
Vegetables and breadsticks for dipping

PREPARATION:

Peel garlic and mince or put through garlic press. Melt butter in a small saucepan. Add garlic and oil. Cook over very low heat 5 minutes until garlic is softened but not browned. Add anchovies and continue cooking 5 minutes. Serve as a dip for breadsticks or for raw or lightly blanched vegetables such as cucumber, fresh mushrooms, celery, zucchini, carrots, cauliflower, green peppers, and green onions.

Variation: Blend 1 cup whipping cream and a generous dash or two freshly ground pepper into garlic-butter mixture. Simmer 2 or 3 minutes. Serve warm.

Makes 1 cup

We are confident that the spirit of the Gilroy Garlic Festival will linger on.

San Jose Mercury

Slender Cheesy Spread

There's little joy in dieting, but if you have a few favorite, low-calorie, standby recipes, you can usually make it through the difficult times when you just "have to have something" without going too far over your calorie limit. Try this cheesy spread with all kinds of vegetables or diet crackers.

Recipe contest entry: Mrs. Gilbert Blakey, San Clemente

---

1 pt. low-fat cottage cheese
3 cloves fresh garlic, minced
1 tbsp. fresh parsley, finely chopped
1 tbsp. mayonnaise
1 tbsp. wine vinegar
Salt and pepper to taste
Celery salt to taste

PREPARATION:

Mix all ingredients together, cover, and refrigerate overnight. Stuff celery, scooped-out small zucchini halves, or spread on crackers or wedges of toast. Sprinkle tops with paprika for added color.

Makes 2 cups

California Crab Dip

California is famous for its garlic and the local Dungeness crab. But you don't have to be a Californian to prepare this unusual and pleasing crabmeat combination. Canned or frozen crabmeat can be substituted if fresh is not available.

1 cup crabmeat (fresh, canned, or frozen)
¼ cup lime juice (or lemon)
1 (3-oz.) package cream cheese
¼ cup heavy cream
2 tbsp. mayonnaise
1 tsp. instant minced onion
1 tsp. minced green onion
1 tsp. Worcestershire sauce
½ tsp. salt
¼ tsp. garlic powder
2 dashes cayenne or red pepper

PREPARATION:
Marinate crabmeat in lime (or lemon) juice 30 minutes. Beat together cream cheese, cream, mayonnaise, and seasonings until smooth and creamy. Fold in marinated crabmeat. Serve in a deep shell or bowl nested in crushed ice. Surround with an arrangement of bite-sized pieces of Chinese cabbage, celery, sliced cauliflowerets, bell pepper strips, and thin slices of carrot. Don't forget a basket of crackers or chips.

Makes about 1½ cups

Marion and Linda's Baked Stuffed Clams

These stuffed clams can be made ahead, frozen, and popped in to the oven just a half-hour before serving time.

Recipe contest entry: Marion Molnar and Linda Hussar, Gilroy

---

8 slices bacon
1½ tbsp. olive oil
3 cloves fresh garlic, minced
2 tbsp. fresh parsley, chopped
⅓ cup plus 2 tbsp. dry breadcrumbs
Pinch of oregano
Dash of pepper
Salt, if necessary, but very little
2 cups chopped clams, fresh-steamed or canned
⅔ cup clam liquid
3 tbsp. grated Parmesan cheese

PREPARATION:
Preheat oven to 350°F. Render fat from bacon, and reserve 1½ tbsp. drippings. Drain bacon on paper towels. Combine drippings and oil in pan and gently sauté garlic, parsley, and onions. Add ⅓ cup breadcrumbs, oregano, pepper, and salt, if needed. Heat no more than 3 minutes. Add clams and clam liquid and mix well. Spoon into individual baking dishes or clean clam shells. Sprinkle with cheese and remaining breadcrumbs. Dust with paprika and sprinkle with pieces of reserved bacon. Bake about 25 minutes or until tops are brown and bacon is crisp (baking time will depend on the serving size). Stuffed clams may be made ahead of time and frozen, then baked 35 minutes before serving.

Makes 4 to 6 servings

Shrimp Appetizer Supreme

This excellent shrimp appetizer could also be served as a main dish with either rice or noodles.

Recipe contest entry: Susan Strommer, Los Angeles

2 lbs. extra-large shrimp
1 tsp. salt
½ tsp. pepper
4 tbsp. lemon juice
3 cloves fresh garlic, crushed
4 tbsp. mayonnaise
1½ cups fine, dry breadcrumbs
1 tsp. crushed basil leaves
2 tsp. chopped parsley
½ tsp. dill weed
½ cup melted butter
4 tbsp. olive oil

PREPARATION:

Preheat oven to 400°F. Shell and devein shrimp. Mix salt, pepper, lemon juice, garlic, and mayonnaise. Stir in shrimp, cover, and refrigerate for 1 to 2 hours. Mix breadcrumbs, basil, parsley, and fill. Coat each shrimp with mixture and place in a single layer on a shallow baking dish. Stir melted butter and olive oil into remaining marinade. Pour over shrimp. Bake for 15 minutes.

Makes 6 to 8 servings

Zucchini Appetizer Angelino

The aroma while this dish bakes is so enticing, your family or guests will be waiting expectantly for their first taste!

Courtesy of: Betty Angelino, Gilroy

4 cups unpeeled zucchini, grated
1¾ cups biscuit mix
¾ cup grated Parmesan cheese
½ cup vegetable oil
4 eggs, beaten
1 large onion, chopped or grated
3 cloves fresh garlic, minced
3 tbsp. minced parsley
½ tsp. salt
½ tsp. crushed oregano

PREPARATION:
Preheat oven to 350°F. Combine all ingredients in a large mixing bowl and stir until well blended. Spread in a greased 13 x 9 x 2 baking dish. Bake for 25 to 30 minutes until golden brown. Cut into bite-sized pieces.
May be served hot or cold.

Makes 48 bite-sized pieces

Parsley-Garlic Finger Sandwiches

Parsley and garlic are good friends because the chlorophyll in the parsley helps to prevent the odor of garlic on the breath. Combined with mayonnaise as a spread, the two herbs make very tasty finger sandwich appetizers.

Recipe contest entry: Mrs. George Parrish, Gilroy

---

2 bunches fresh parsley, finely chopped
2 large cloves fresh garlic, pressed
½ cup mayonnaise
1 loaf white bread, crusts removed, sliced extra-thin (20 slices)

PREPARATION:
Combine parsley, garlic, and mayonnaise; mix well. Spread mixture between two slices of bread and cut diagonally to make 4 finger sandwiches. Refrigerate until ready to serve. These can be made early on the day they are to be served, but *not* the day before.

Makes 80 sandwiches

Linda Tarvin's recipe for Garlic Toothpaste for Yellow and/or Stained Teeth didn't make it to the Great Garlic Cook-off finals. It called for 20 cloves of garlic. However, the toothpaste recipe did provide a few laughs for the committee sorting the 500-plus entries. And that was the retired teacher's intent. "Does not remove yellow or stain from teeth but nobody will ever get close enough to notice," says Mrs. Tarvin.

Mary Phillips, *San Jose Mercury*

Zucchini and Mushroom Hors d'Oeuvres

With everyone trying to eat more nutritious foods and avoid "empty calories," this healthful, delicious, and simple-to-prepare hors d'oeuvre should help make you a popular host or hostess.

Recipe contest entry: Linda Tarvin, Morgan Hill

½ cup butter or margarine
4 cloves fresh garlic, minced
2 tbsp. chopped fresh parsley
Pepper to taste
1 lb. mushroom caps
2 medium zucchini, sliced ¼ inch thick
Grated Parmesan cheese
Paprika

PREPARATION:
Preheat broiler. Combine butter, garlic, and parsley in a saucepan over low heat and cook until bubbly. Add pepper to taste. Cover and chill slightly until the mixture is not runny. Arrange mushroom caps (cup-side up), and zucchini slices on serving dishes. Top each with ¼ teaspoon garlic-butter mixture. Sprinkle with Parmesan cheese and paprika. Cook for 2 to 4 minutes under broiler until bubbly.

Makes about 40 to 50 hors d'oeuvres

Escargots Carmela

What garlic cookbook would be complete without a recipe for garlic-buttered snails? This variation was an entry in the First Great Recipe Contest and Cook-off. You might try a light sprinkling of Parmesan cheese on each snail before baking. Serve with plenty of hot French bread to sop up the garlic butter!

Recipe contest entry: Carmela M. Meely, Walnut Creek

---

4 oz. butter, softened
1 tbsp. chopped fresh parsley
3 cloves fresh garlic, minced
1 minced shallot
Pepper
Salt
Pinch ground nutmeg
1 tbsp. white wine or champagne
12 snails and shells

PREPARATION:
Preheat oven to 350°F. Cream butter. Add all ingredients except snails, and mix until well blended. Arrange shells on baking sheet. Place a dab of butter mixture into each shell. Add snails to shells and cover each with a dollop of butter mixture. Bake for 10 minutes. Serve hot.

Makes 12 snails; 4 per person

Italian Sausage-Stuffed Mushrooms

Italians everywhere love their mushrooms. Some like them best as an appetizer stuffed with garlic and Italian sausage.

Recipe contest entry: Carmela M. Meely, Walnut Creek

---

18 to 20 large mushrooms
½ lb. Italian sausage (regular or fennel, bulk type)
½ cup chopped onion
3 cloves fresh garlic, minced
2 tbsp. olive oil
¼ cup breadcrumbs
1 egg
¼ cup grated Parmesan cheese
Additional Parmesan cheese for garnish

PREPARATION:

Preheat oven to 350°F. Remove stems from mushrooms. Chop stems. Brown sausage, onion, garlic and chopped stems in oil. Drain well. Cool. Mix with breadcrumbs, egg, and cheese. Stuff mushrooms caps. Bake for 15 to 20 minutes. Sprinkle with extra Parmesan.

Makes 18 to 20 mushrooms; 4 to 5 per person

Garlic Mushrooms Morgan Hill

Linda was among the Top Ten finalists in the First Great Garlic Recipe Contest and Cook-off. Her mushroom recipe drew raves, not only for its flavor, but for its attractive presentation with whole garlic bulbs used as decoration.

Recipe contest finalist: Linda Tarvin, Morgan Hill

---

4 cloves fresh garlic, minced
⅓ cup olive oil
⅔ cup white wine vinegar
⅓ cup dry red or white wine
2 tbsp. soy sauce
2 tbsp. honey
2 tbsp. chopped parsley
1 tbsp. salt
2 lbs. fresh mushrooms

PREPARATION:

Sauté garlic in oil. Add vinegar, wine, soy sauce, honey, parsley, and salt. Stir until mixture is well blended and hot. Place mushrooms in a heat-proof container with a tightly fitting lid. Pour hot mixture over mushrooms; allow to marinate from 1 to 3 hours, or more, turning over several times. Save marinade for later use on more mushrooms or use as a salad dressing.

Makes enough to marinate 50 to 60 mushrooms

Artichoke Hearts Marinati

From nearby Castroville come the artichoke hearts for this popular Italian antipasto. Whole artichokes may also be steamed or boiled until tender, the marinade spooned over them and chilled for about 6 hours, then served cold.

1 (9-oz.) package frozen artichoke hearts
2 tbsp. lemon juice
1 tbsp. olive oil
¾ tsp. garlic salt
¼ tsp. oregano leaves
¼ tsp. chervil leaves
¼ tsp. tarragon leaves

PREPARATION:
Cook artichoke hearts following directions on package. Drain and put in a small bowl. Combine remaining ingredients and pour over artichoke hearts. Chill at least 2 hours before serving.

Makes about 1½ cups

Rose Emma's Eggplant Relish

Eggplant is a very versatile vegetable and it's at its best when flavored with garlic, onions, and tomatoes.

Courtesy of: Rose Emma Pelliccione, Gilroy

---

3 cups eggplant, peeled and cut into ½-inch cubes
⅓ cup chopped green peppers
1 medium onion, minced
3 cloves garlic, pressed
⅓ cup oil
1 (6-oz.) can tomato paste
1 (4-oz.) can mushroom stems and pieces
½ cup pimiento-stuffed olives
¼ cup water
2 tbsp. red wine vinegar
1½ tsp. sugar
1 tsp. seasoned salt
½ tsp. oregano
¼ tsp. pepper

PREPARATION:

Put eggplant, green pepper, onion, garlic, and oil in a skillet. Cover and cook gently for 10 minutes, stirring occasionally. Add tomato paste, mushrooms with liquid, and remaining ingredients. Cover and simmer 30 minutes. Turn into a covered dish and refrigerate overnight to allow flavors to blend. Serve with crackers and chips.

Makes about 4 cups (1 quart)

Creamy Garlic-Herb Cheese

Creamy-rich and delightfully herbed, Boursin cheese is a favorite spread for crackers. Here's an easy homemade version that captures a similar flavor.

Recipe contest entry: Julie and Gary Crites, La Verne

---

2 (8-oz.) packages cream cheese
1 pint sour cream
½ cup butter
3 cloves fresh garlic, pressed
¼ cup snipped chives

PREPARATION:
Mix all ingredients in a blender or food processor. Cover and chill in refrigerator several hours. Warm to room temperature before serving with crackers or as a dip for fresh raw vegetables.

Makes about 4 cups (1 quart)

Rubino's Stuffed Mushrooms

Rancher/chef Jim Rubino shares his recipe for the stuffed mushrooms that were a hit at the Festival's Gourmet Alley. These mushrooms make great finger appetizers for company, but don't forget your family too. Prepare them the day before or at the last minute, but be sure to make plenty because they'll quickly disappear.

Courtesy of: Jim Rubino, San Martin

1 cup butter
⅓ cup crushed garlic
1 lb. grated Parmesan cheese
⅓ cup chopped parsley
50 large mushrooms

PREPARATION:
Preheat broiler. Brush mushrooms clean, and remove stems. Melt butter, stir in crushed garlic, grated cheese, and parsley. Stuff each mushroom cap. Place mushrooms on broiler pan, stuffing-side up, and broil until tops turn golden brown. Serve hot out of the broiler!

Makes 50 mushrooms; 4 to 5 per person

The main attraction was the cooking contest and it was a doozy. The winners were real winners.

Food and Wine Magazine

Mock Caviar

Simulate the real thing with this imaginative imitation nestled in an iced bowl.
Serve with lemon, finely chopped eggs, tomato, and onion.

1981 Recipe contest finalist: Barry Wertz, British Columbia, Canada

3 large cloves fresh garlic
1 (2-oz.) can anchovies
2 cups chopped black olives
2 large ripe avocados

PREPARATION:
Peel and crush garlic. Drain and mash anchovies. Drain olives and mash avocados. Combine all ingredients. Turn into an iced bowl. Serve as a spread for thin crackers or toast. *Note:* To store, squeeze lemon juice over top, seal tightly with clear plastic wrap, and refrigerate.

Makes 3 cups

The festival of harvest is, of course, a unifying event as old as civilization itself, but to do it well is the equivalent of staging an opera or anything else that lifts the spirit. In this regard, Gilroy is approaching the first rank.

San Francisco Examiner

Garlic-Chicken Filo Rolls

Flaky, golden sheets of filo dough encase tender, moist chicken, prosciutto, garlic, and cheese in this Mediterranean inspired recipe.

1981 Recipe contest finalist: Mary Jane Himel, Palo Alto

2 bulbs fresh garlic (approximately 30 cloves)
½ cup dry white wine
½ cup water
Juice of 1 lemon
¼ tsp. salt
1 lb. boneless, skinless chicken breasts
6 sheets filo, defrosted
¼ cup butter, melted
2½ oz. thinly sliced prosciutto or 3 slices boiled ham, halved
2 cups grated Swiss cheese

PREPARATION:
Preheat oven to 400°F. Separate garlic into cloves and drop into boiling water. Simmer 1 minute, drain, and peel. Bring wine, water, lemon juice, and salt to a simmer in a large saucepan. Add the chicken and garlic. Cook at a bare simmer, turning occasionally, just until chicken is cooked. Remove chicken and continue cooking garlic until tender, then drain. Cut chicken into large chunks and divide into 6 portions. Lay out 1 filo sheet, brush half of it with butter, and fold in half crosswise. Brush with butter again. Top with a portion of chicken along a short end. Top with ⅙ of the garlic cloves, lightly mashed with a fork, ⅙ of the prosciutto, and ⅓ cup cheese. Fold in the sides and roll up. Repeat with remaining filo sheets. Work quickly so filo doesn't dry out. Place rolls on lightly greased baking sheet and brush them with butter. Bake about 20 minutes, until golden.

Makes 6 rolls

Vegetables, Salads, and Dressings

"Wel loved he garleek, onyons and eek lekes," it was said in Chaucer's *Canterbury Tales*, and still these pungent bulbs continue to be enjoyed for their satisfying aroma and the zesty flavor they impart. Vegetable dishes respond particularly well to the addition of garlic during preparation, whether they are steamed, baked, stir-fried, or combined in such spectacular dishes as Gilroy Ratatouille or Hollister Vegetable Casserole. And when it comes to salads, what dressing is not improved by the addition of garlic? We know of none.

Quick and Easy Recipe Ideas

Perk up frozen spinach with garlic. Simply cook spinach in a little water until thawed, then add pressed fresh garlic cloves and butter. Heat just until done.

Cook green beans in wine for real flavor enhancement. Partially steam the beans, then cook in white wine, fresh minced garlic and butter.

Give Quiche Lorraine a sassy twist by adding fresh minced garlic to the filling.

Potatoes go from ordinary to extraordinary when fried with minced fresh garlic cloves. Season with garlic salt and sprinkle with grated cheese.

When cooking vegetables, add some sliced fresh garlic cloves to the cooking water to impart subtle flavor.

Here's a basic formula for salad dressing: Combine 3 parts oil with 1 part vinegar or lemon juice. Season with salt, freshly ground pepper, and one or more cloves of crushed fresh garlic. Shake well in a screw-top jar and let stand for a few hours to blend flavors. Remove garlic before serving. Vary the basic dressing by adding other herbs and spices.

For discreet garlic flavor in your salad, rub halved cloves of fresh garlic on a crust of bread (called a *chapon* in French), then wipe the salad bowl with the bread before adding greens.

Garlicky Mushrooms Supreme

Use this great mushroom dish as a vegetable side dish at your next dinner party.

Recipe contest entry: Carrie Cohen, Woodland Hills

---

1 lb. fresh mushrooms, sliced
4 tbsp. olive oil
7 cloves fresh garlic, sliced
3 tbsp. chopped parsley
Salt and pepper to taste

PREPARATION:

Sauté mushrooms in olive oil, covered, about 15 minutes. Uncover, and add garlic, parsley, salt, and pepper. Simmer until liquid evaporates. Do not allow garlic to brown. Serve and enjoy.

Makes 4 servings

Ali Baba's Carrots

This cold vegetable side dish is perfect with a summer meal of barbecued meat, beans, and potato salad. It can be made a day or two ahead, which actually improves its flavor.

Recipe contest entry: Phyllis Gaddis, Venice

2 lbs. carrots
Boiling water
6 tbsp. water or chicken broth
6 tbsp. olive oil
7 cloves fresh garlic
3 tbsp. tarragon or white wine vinegar

½ tsp. dill weed
¼ tsp. cayenne
¼ tsp. paprika
¼ tsp. cumin
2 tbsp. chopped parsley

PREPARATION:

Peel carrots and cut into 2-inch pieces. Blanch in boiling water for one minute, then plunge into a bowl of cold water. After two minutes, remove from cold water and drain. Meanwhile, in a saucepan, heat water or chicken broth with olive oil, 2 whole cloves garlic, and salt and pepper to taste. Bring to a boil, then add carrots. Lower heat and simmer until tender but firm. Drain carrots, reserving liquid and whole garlic cloves. In a glass or plastic bowl large enough to hold carrots, mix marinade by combining vinegar, dill weed, cayenne, paprika, cumin, 5 garlic cloves (minced), and salt and pepper to taste. Add remaining garlic cloves and the reserved liquid. Cover and chill in refrigerator at least 6 hours (or as long as a day or two). To serve, drain carrots from marinade and place in dish. Sprinkle with chopped parsley.

Makes 6 servings

Basque-style Eggplant Casserole

The Basques of northern Spain and southwestern France are noted for serving foods with robust flavor. They love their garlic, too!

6 tbsp. oil
1 onion, sliced into rings
2 green peppers, cut into strips
5 large mushrooms, sliced
1 celery stalk, sliced diagonally
5 cloves fresh garlic, minced
6 tomatoes, peeled and diced
Salt to taste
1 tbsp. fines herbes
1 large eggplant
2 eggs, beaten with 1 tbsp. water and pinch of salt
½ cup freshly grated Parmesan cheese
1 cup grated Swiss cheese

PREPARATION:

Preheat oven to 350°F. Heat 3 tbsp. oil in a large skillet; add onion, green peppers, mushrooms, celery, and garlic. Sauté until tender. Add tomatoes. Bring to a boil. Add salt and fines herbes. Turn heat to low and simmer for 30 minutes. Peel eggplant and slice into ½-inch slices. Dip in egg mixture and fry eggplant in a skillet with remaining oil until tender. Arrange eggplant slices in a large baking dish. Sprinkle with Parmesan cheese. Pour tomato sauce over the top and sprinkle with Swiss cheese. Heat in oven until cheese is melted.

Makes 4 servings

China Camp Stir-fried Vegetables

Without fresh garlic, stir-fry vegetables might be good but not great. This combination is the greatest!

2 tbsp. oil
4 cloves fresh garlic
2 lbs. vegetables cut into ½-inch diagonal slices
   (asparagus, broccoli, green beans, etc.)
1 (8-oz.) can water chestnuts, drained and sliced
2 tbsp. soy sauce
Salt and pepper to taste
¼ cup toasted nuts, if desired (peanuts, almonds, cashews, etc.)

PREPARATION:
Heat oil in a large skillet or wok. Smash garlic by whacking cloves with butt of a knife handle. Remove peel. Add garlic to oil. When garlic becomes aromatic, remove and discard. Add vegetables and stir-fry over high heat until crisp-tender. Add water chestnuts, soy sauce, salt, and pepper. Stir-fry 1 minute more to heat through. Sprinkle with nuts and serve at once.

Makes 4 to 6 servings

Snow Peas Canton

The Chinese have had a strong influence on California's history as well as its cuisine, and who knows better than the Chinese how to combine vegetables and garlic into mouth-watering dishes like this one!

1 tbsp. peanut oil
4 to 5 cloves fresh garlic, minced
½ lb. Chinese pea pods, ends trimmed, strings removed
1 (5-oz.) can bamboo shoots, drained
1 (8-oz.) can water chestnuts, drained and sliced
¼ cup canned or fresh chicken broth
2 tsp. soy sauce
1 tsp. cornstarch
2 tsp. water

PREPARATION:

Heat oil in a large skillet or wok. Sauté garlic until light brown. Add peas, bamboo shoots, and water chestnuts. Stir-fry 1 minute. Add chicken broth and soy sauce. Cover and cook 1 minute more. In a small bowl, combine cornstarch and water. Stir into skillet. Cook over high heat until sauce thickens and appears glossy, about 1 minute.

Makes 4 servings

Greek Beans

The Greeks are masters of seasoning with garlic. This dish is particularly easy to prepare, but good enough for company!

Recipe contest entry: Barbara Flory, South Laguna

1 lb. fresh green beans
1 cup tomato juice
¼ cup olive oil
3 cloves fresh garlic, pressed
3 tomatoes, cut into quarters
1 chopped onion
½ cup chopped parsley
½ tsp. crushed oregano leaves
½ tsp. paprika
1 tsp. garlic salt
Salt and pepper to taste

PREPARATION:

Cut beans into thirds. Cook in tomato juice over medium-low heat until tender. Meanwhile, in the olive oil, sauté garlic, tomatoes, onion, parsley, and oregano until tender but still crisp. When beans are tender, add sautéed ingredients, paprika, garlic salt, and salt and pepper to taste. Simmer 5 minutes, then serve immediately.

Makes 4 servings

Hollister Vegetable Casserole

A finalist in the Great Garlic Recipe Contest and Cook-off, Lena says this entry is a favorite with her family and some of the Gavilan College staff where she is cafeteria manager. "This dish is particularly good for vegetarians," says Lena. It would also be a good choice as a side dish to serve with barbecued meats.

Recipe contest finalist: Lena Lico, Hollister

6 zucchini, sliced
6 potatoes, peeled and sliced
3 bell peppers, cut in strips
2 large onions, sliced
1 large eggplant, sliced
½ cup Romano or Parmesan cheese
Salt and pepper to taste
5 cloves fresh garlic, pressed
1 tsp. oregano
8 large tomatoes, sliced, or 2 lbs. canned tomatoes, sliced
½ cup oil

PREPARATION:
Preheat oven to 350°F. Place layers of vegetables in greased baking pan alternating with 4 tbsp. grated cheese, salt, and oregano with tomatoes. Top the casserole with tomatoes and 4 tbsp. cheese. Drizzle oil over top. Cover and bake for 1½ hours. Uncover and bake at 375°F for another 1½ hours.

Makes 4 to 6 servings

Artichoke and Carrot Frittata

This vegetable frittata is excellent served as an evening meal or a brunch. It could be topped with white sauce and garnished with sliced ripe olives or served on bread as a sandwich filling.

Recipe contest entry: Fanny Cimoli, San Jose

---

2 cups sliced or chopped cooked artichoke hearts
8 eggs, beaten
1 cup grated cheese (Italian or American)
1 cup grated carrot
½ cup finely chopped parsley
½ cup chopped onion
⅛ cup chopped celery
5 cloves fresh garlic, minced
1 tbsp. catsup
1 tsp. salt
¼ tsp. pepper
Garlic salt to taste

PREPARATION:

Preheat oven to 300°F. Combine all ingredients together and blend well. Pour into 9 x 11 baking dish, lightly greased. Bake for 20 to 30 minutes until golden brown. Do not overbake, as it may become dry. Cut into squares and serve.

Makes 6 to 8 servings

Garlic Butter Crumb Tomatoes

Karen Christopher, wife of Gilroy garlic grower and shipper Don Christopher, says, "I'm not a person who enjoys long hours in the kitchen, but I always serve dishes laced with fresh garlic. This recipe for crumb-topped tomatoes is fast and easy. A perfect choice for a second vegetable."

Courtesy of: Karen Christopher

---

4 fresh ripe tomatoes
½ cup seasoned dry breadcrumbs
4 tbsp. melted butter
2 large cloves fresh garlic, minced
½ tsp. basil
Salt and pepper to taste
Fresh minced garlic
Minced parsley for garnish

PREPARATION:
Preheat broiler. Cut tomatoes into halves and arrange on baking dish or tray. Combine breadcrumbs with melted butter, garlic, basil, salt, and pepper. Spread crumb mixture on tomato halves and place in broiler 10 inches from heat until browned. Garnish with remaining minced garlic and parsley and serve.

Makes 4 servings

Eggplant Parmigiana

This famous Italian dish takes full advantage of the wonderful flavor combination of garlic, tomatoes, and Parmesan cheese.

2 medium eggplants
Oil for frying
1 (6-oz.) can tomato paste
¾ tsp. garlic powder
1½ tsp. seasoned salt
⅛ tsp. black pepper
1 tbsp. parsley flakes
1 bay leaf
½ cup grated Parmesan cheese
2 cups soft breadcrumbs
½ lb. sliced Mozzarella cheese

PREPARATION:

Preheat oven to 350°F. Peel eggplant and cut into ½-inch slices. Sauté in oil 5 minutes or until tender and lightly browned. Remove and keep warm. In a skillet combine tomatoes, tomato paste, garlic powder, seasoned salt, pepper, parsley flakes. and bay leaf. Cover and simmer 15 minutes. Remove bay leaf; add Parmesan cheese and breadcrumbs, mixing well. Place a layer of eggplant in buttered, shallow 2-quart baking dish. Cover with half the tomato sauce, then with half the Mozzarella cheese. Repeat layers. Bake 20 minutes or until cheese melts and is lightly browned. Serve at once with some crusty sourdough bread.

Makes 5 to 6 servings

Val and Elsie's Julienne Beans

Val Filice, garlic grower and head chef of Gourmet Alley, and his wife Elsie glamorize canned beans when cooking at home!

Courtesy of: Val and Elsie Filice, Gilroy

4 cloves fresh garlic, crushed
1 bacon strip, cut crosswise into ¼ inch strips
4 tbsp. olive oil
3 (1-lb.) cans julienne-style green beans
¼ cup liquid reserved after draining beans
1 tsp. dry oregano
1 tsp. dry basil (or fresh)
Salt and pepper to taste

PREPARATION:
Sauté garlic and bacon in olive oil until garlic turns amber in color. Remove pan from heat and add beans, liquid, herbs, and salt and pepper and cook over medium heat until beans are warmed through.

Makes 6 to 8 servings

Zesty Zucchini Sauté

A quick and tasty way to serve zucchini, this dish goes well with any meat.

4 medium zucchini
2 tsp. seasoned salt
2 tsp. parsley flakes
1 tsp. dried minced onion
½ tsp. ground oregano
¼ tsp. garlic powder
¼ tsp. pepper
¼ cup olive oil

PREPARATION:
Wash zucchini but do not peel. Slice in rounds about ¼-inch thick. In a mixing bowl, combine remaining ingredients except olive oil. Sprinkle over zucchini and toss until seasoning is well distributed. Heat oil in skillet; add zucchini and sauté until browned on both sides, about 10 minutes. Drain on paper towels.

Makes 4 servings

Cauliflower with Garlic Oil

This unusual treatment gives cauliflower a delightfully different flavor.

1 head cauliflower or broccoli
1 cup olive oil
½ tsp. salt
4 cloves fresh garlic, minced
1 tbsp. chopped parsley
3 hard-boiled eggs, chopped

PREPARATION:

Separate cauliflower into florets and steam in a small amount of water or in steamer basket until crisp-tender. Drain and set aside in warmed serving dish. Heat oil and salt in a small pan and cook garlic and parsley until garlic is lightly browned. Pour oil mixture over cauliflower and garnish with chopped eggs.

Makes 4 servings

Stuffed Artichokes Castroville

The garlic and Parmesan cheese, classic flavor mates, make these stuffed artichokes a very special dish and very popular, not only in Gilroy, but throughout the West.

Recipe contest entry: Mikki DeDominic, Guerneville

---

6 or 8 small artichokes
½ cup breadcrumbs
½ cup grated Parmesan cheese
5 cloves fresh garlic
2 tbsp. parsley
Salt and pepper to taste
Olive oil

PREPARATION:
Clean outer leaves of artichokes and cut the tops and bottoms so they are flat. Scoop out choke, if desired. Mix breadcrumbs, cheese, 3 cloves of garlic (minced), parsley, salt and pepper. Spread the leaves of artichokes and fill in every leaf with the bread mixture, including the center of the artichoke. In a low saucepan large enough to hold artichokes, heat 1 tbsp. of oil and sauté remaining 2 cloves garlic (minced) until the garlic is slightly brown. Stand artichokes in the pan and fill pan with water about 1-inch deep. (Water level depends on the size of the artichokes—do not allow water to reach breadcrumb stuffing.) Cover pan with aluminum foil to allow artichokes to steam. Cook until tender. If water evaporates before artichokes are tender, add more water.

Makes 6 to 8 servings

Capered Carrots and Zucchini

Two ordinary vegetables become special when sautéed with garlic and rosemary. Capers add an elegant touch and a spicy flavor.

Recipe contest entry: Angie Herrera, Norwalk

5 medium carrots
3 small zucchini
2 tbsp. butter
3 cloves fresh garlic, minced
Pinch rosemary
Salt and pepper
Water
1 tbsp. capers

PREPARATION:

Slice carrots and zucchini about ¼-inch thick. Melt butter in frying pan over medium heat; lightly sauté garlic, then stir in carrots and cook 2 minutes. Stir in zucchini, rosemary, salt and pepper to taste. Stir until zucchini is heated through, then add 1 or 2 tbsp. water and cover pan. Cook over medium heat until carrots are barely fork-tender, shaking pan, and stirring occasionally. Don't overcook. Stir in capers and serve.

Makes 4 servings

Zucchini alla Pelliccione

Served as a cold side dish or salad, this minty marinated zucchini dish from a Gourmet Alley chef is an unusual accompaniment for almost any meal.

Courtesy of: Paul Pelliccione, Gilroy

7 to 8 zucchini (not over 2½-inch diameter)
Salt
2 cups flour
2 cups vegetable oil
3 cups dry breadcrumbs
30 fresh garlic slices (6 to 8 cloves)
30 fresh mint leaves
Wine vinegar

PREPARATION:

Wash zucchini and trim ends. Slice uniformly to ³⁄₁₆-inch thickness. Arrange one layer in a colander and sprinkle with salt. Continue with layers, sprinkling each with salt until all slices have been used. Let stand for 1 hour. Roll slices in flour to coat and set aside. Heat oil to 300°F in a large skillet. Fry slices on both sides until they barely begin to brown. Set aside on a cookie sheet to cool completely. Place layer of sliced zucchini in a large bowl. Sprinkle generously with bread-crumbs. Arrange some of the garlic slices and mint leaves over the crumbs. Sprinkle generously with wine vinegar. Continue to layer zucchini and other ingredients in this order until all ingredients are used. Cover and refrigerate.

Makes 4 to 6 servings

Tomatoes à la Clare

"Delicious *and* pretty," says the woman who entered this recipe in the Great Garlic Recipe Contest. We have to agree.

Recipe contest entry: Clara M. Lutz, Redondo Beach

---

6 medium to large tomatoes, sliced
3 cloves fresh garlic, minced
1 bunch green onions, minced (include some green tops)
⅓ cup minced parsley
½ tsp. salt
Coarse black pepper to taste
⅓ cup corn oil
¼ cup brown cider vinegar
1 tbsp. Dijon mustard

PREPARATION:
Arrange tomatoes in a shallow dish or platter. Mix garlic, onions, parsley, salt, and pepper; sprinkle over tomatoes. Cover with plastic wrap and refrigerate 3 to 4 hours. Prepare dressing by combining oil, vinegar, and mustard. At serving time, shake well and pour over tomatoes.

Makes 4 to 6 servings

Gilroy Ratatouille

Enhanced by sausage and cheese, this ratatouille makes a complete meal. For vegetarians, just omit the sausage.

Recipe contest entry: Mrs. Gene Stecyk, Los Angeles

3 cloves fresh garlic, minced
2 onions, thinly sliced
⅓ cup olive oil
1 green pepper, cut into thin rounds
2 medium eggplant, diced, unpeeled
2 medium zucchini, sliced ¼ inch thick
1 (20-oz.) can whole Italian tomatoes
1½ tsp. basil
1½ tsp. parsley
1½ tsp. salt
Fresh ground pepper to taste
1½ lbs. Italian sausage, sliced
½ lb. whole mushrooms
1 cup grated Swiss cheese

PREPARATION:

Sauté garlic and onions in oil until soft. Add green pepper, eggplant, and zucchini and cook 5 minutes over medium heat, tossing constantly. Add tomatoes with liquid and seasonings. Lower heat and simmer uncovered 15 minutes, then cover and simmer 15 minutes more. Meanwhile, cook sausage in frying pan until done and drain well. Add mushrooms to vegetables during last 10 minutes of cooking time. Add sausage to vegetables. Sprinkle with grated cheese. Cover and simmer until cheese melts.

Makes 8 servings

Vegetables Veracruz

Inspired by the classic Mexican sauce for red snapper, this vegetable dish has a flavor all its own.

Recipe contest entry: Norman Simmons, Los Angeles

1 whole bulb fresh garlic
1 medium eggplant (approx. 1½ lbs.)
2 small zucchini
1½ tsp. salt
½ tsp. ascorbic acid (or fruit canning mix)
1 medium onion
¼ cup olive oil
 2 tbsp. butter
1 tsp. oregano
1 tsp. sweet basil
¼ tsp. pepper
1 (28-oz.) can whole peeled tomatoes
1 tsp. cornstarch mixed with 1 tbsp. water

PREPARATION:

Separate the garlic cloves and remove skins. Peel and cut eggplant into ¾-inch cubes. Cut zucchini into ¾-inch rounds and then into quarters. Place zucchini and eggplant in a bowl and cover with water in which 1 tsp. salt and the ascorbic acid have been dissolved. Weight down and let stand while preparing remaining ingredients. Cut onion in half, then quarters, and slice thinly. Reserve 4 garlic cloves and gently sauté the remainder with onions in oil and butter over low heat for 10 minutes. Add oregano, basil, ½ tsp. salt, pepper, and the drained liquid from the tomatoes. Seed the drained tomatoes, cut them into

¾-inch pieces, and set aside. Steam zucchini and eggplant for 10 minutes. When done, add to the onion-garlic mixture along with the tomatoes. Mince reserved garlic cloves and add to vegetables. Raise heat and add the cornstarch in water, stirring until thickened and glazed. Simmer 5 minutes more and remove. Do not overcook. Let stand to blend flavors. This is delicious served hot or cold, and even better the next day.

Makes 6 servings

Green Beans Asadoor

There must be a thousand ways to serve green beans. This one has a wonderful Italian flavor.

Recipe contest entry: Virginia Asadoor, Pasadena

1 cup chopped onions
4 cloves fresh garlic
4 oz. butter or margarine
4 tbsp. tomato sauce
1 tsp. sweet basil
1 lb. fresh green beans

PREPARATION:
Sauté onions and garlic in butter. Add tomato sauce and basil. Place green beans over onions and garlic. Cover and simmer until cooked (approximately 15 to 20 minutes).

Makes 4 servings

Dilled Green Beans

It is always nice to have something homemade on the shelf to bring out to complete a party meal or take as a house gift next time you visit friends. These dill-and-garlic-flavored green beans would be welcome anywhere.

2 lbs. green beans (young and tender)
1 tsp. powdered alum
1 gallon water
4 tsp. dill seed
2 tsp. mustard seed
1 tsp. crushed red pepper
½ tsp. dehydrated minced garlic
2 cups water
2 cups vinegar
¼ cup salt

PREPARATION:

Wash beans and trim ends; place in a stone crock or glass container. Dissolve alum in the 1 gallon water; pour over beans and let stand 24 hours. Drain and wash. Put beans in saucepan and add about 1 cup water. Cover and boil 5 minutes, then drain. Pack beans lengthwise in 4 sterilized canning jars. To each jar add 1 tsp. dill seed, ½ tsp. mustard seed, ¼ tsp. crushed red pepper, and ⅛ tsp. dehydrated garlic. Combine remaining ingredients and bring to a boil. Pour over beans, leaving ¼-inch head space. Seal jars at once.

Makes 4 jars beans

The Gubsers' Green Bean and Garlic Frittata

Joseph Gubser's father began growing garlic in Gilroy in the 1920s and to put it in Joe's words, "I grew up with the industry." This grower/shipper and his wife, Doris, have contributed this unusual and tasty treatment for beans. It can be served as a cold vegetable dish or as an hors d'oeuvre.

Courtesy of: Joseph and Doris Gubser, Gilroy

1 green pepper, chopped
1 small onion, chopped
¼ cup plus 3 tbsp. olive oil
3 lbs. canned green beans, drained
¾ cup breadcrumbs
½ cup grated Parmesan cheese plus additional cheese for topping
¼ cup sherry
3 eggs, beaten
3 large cloves fresh garlic, minced
1 tbsp. Italian seasoning
¼ tsp. salt
⅛ tsp. pepper
Paprika

PREPARATION:

Sauté pepper and onion in 3 tbsp. olive oil. Combine with beans and all other ingredients (except paprika and cheese reserved for topping) into buttered (2-quart) baking dish. Sprinkle with additional grated Parmesan and paprika. Serve cold as a vegetable dish or as an hors d'oeuvre.

Makes 10 to 12 servings

Baked Garlic Potatoes

The goodness of garlic and the popular appeal of potatoes makes this dish a winning combination. Small unpeeled potatoes are baked whole in a casserole and drizzled with garlic-flavored oil.

1 lb. small white potatoes (about 1½ inches in diameter)
4 cloves fresh garlic, minced
4 tbsp. olive oil
¼ cup chopped parsley
2 tsp. coarse salt
¼ tsp. freshly ground pepper
Butter or margarine

PREPARATION:

Preheat oven to 450°F. Wash and dry potatoes; arrange in a casserole in two layers. Combine garlic, oil, parsley, salt and pepper. Pour over potatoes and toss to coat with oil mixture. Cover and bake for 20 minutes. Turn potatoes to recoat in oil, then bake another 25 minutes. Cut potatoes open and squeeze ends to fluff them up. Serve with butter or margarine.

Makes 6 servings

Light 'n Lovely Eggplant Casserole

A different kind of eggplant dish, this recipe requires no cheese and no preliminary frying of the eggplant. It's great for low-fat diets.

Recipe contest entry: Joseph Noury, Sunnyvale

4 large eggplants
3 large onions, diced
1 cup diced celery
5 cloves fresh garlic, minced
2 lbs. ground chuck
2 (16-oz.) cans tomatoes
1 (6-oz.) can tomato paste
1½ tsp. allspice

PREPARATION:

Preheat oven to 350°F. Cut eggplant into slices about ⅜-inch thick. Salt each slice and place in a colander to drain. Combine onion, celery, garlic, and ground meat in a large pan. Brown all together, drain off fat, and let cool. In a saucepan crush tomatoes and combine with tomato paste and allspice. Bring to a slow boil for 15 minutes and then simmer for ½ hour. Let cool before using. Rinse off eggplant. Cover the bottom of a 10 x 13 x 2 baking pan with 1 cup tomato sauce mixture. Layer pan with eggplant, meat, and tomato mixture. You should be able to make three layers. Add meat and sauce on top layer. Cover with foil and bake for ½ hour. Reduce heat to 300°F for ½ hour; remove foil and bake another 15 minutes. Serve over steamed rice.

Makes 6 to 8 servings

Queen's Beans

This easy-to-fix vegetable dish can be a hearty meal-in-one with the addition of ham, ham hocks, or hamburger.

Recipe contest entry: Mrs. Gil (Queen) Murphy, San Diego

1 lb. small white beans
7 cups cold water
1 tsp. salt
¼ tsp. paprika
2 large onions, quartered
½ cup tomato sauce
10 large cloves fresh garlic, halved
½ cup parsley sprigs
¼ cup olive roil

PREPARATION:

Cook beans in water for 1 hour. Add salt, paprika, and onions. Cover and cook 1 hour. Add tomato sauce, garlic, parsley, and olive oil. Cook 30 minutes longer. Serve with lemon juice.

Makes 8 servings

Garlic Mushroom Casserole

Plump, fresh mushrooms are stuffed with a hardy filling that includes plenty of garlic and a surprise ingredient: chopped almonds. For a vegetarian meal prepare it with a soy paste as a substitute for the beef.

1980 Recipe contest finalist: R. J. Harris, Gilroy

16 large fresh mushrooms for stuffing
½ lb. small mushrooms
1 cup finely diced fresh garlic
1 cup chopped almonds
½ lb. butter
1 lb. ground beef
2 cups seasoned breadcrumbs
1 cup grated Swiss or Mozzarella cheese
½ cup grated Parmesan cheese

PREPARATION:

Preheat oven to 350°F. Clean large mushrooms. Remove stems and chop together with small mushrooms. Sauté garlic, chopped mushrooms, and almonds in half the butter. Add beef and cook until done. Add 1½ cups breadcrumbs and mix thoroughly.

Line bottom of greased casserole with 8 large mushrooms, open-side up. Stuff sautéed mixture firmly into mushrooms. Use remaining 8 large mushrooms to cover sautéed mixture (place open-side down). Sprinkle with grated Swiss or Mozzarella cheese, remaining breadcrumbs and Parmesan cheese. Dot with remaining half of the butter and bake for 35 minutes or until mushrooms are tender. *Note:* Use soy paste instead of ground meat. Add extra ½ lb. butter for moisture.

Makes 8 servings

Garlic Shrimp Salad

Delicate pink shrimp with luscious green avocados and artichoke hearts are featured in this salad, an adaptation of one served all around the Mediterranean. For variation, chicken can be substituted for the shrimp.

1981 Recipe contest finalist: Lovelle Oberholzer, Concord

9 cloves fresh garlic
¼ cup butter or margarine
1½ to 2 lbs. large shrimp,
   shelled and deveined
2 large tomatoes
2 medium cucumbers
3 green onions

4 cooked artichoke hearts, halved
½ cup vegetable oil
¼ cup lemon juice
½ tsp. crushed sweet basil
¼ tsp. dried dill weed
Salt and pepper
1 ripe avocado

PREPARATION:

Peel and mince 6 cloves garlic. Melt butter in a heavy skillet. Add minced garlic and sauté over medium heat until light golden. Add shrimp and cook 2 or 3 minutes, turning continuously, just until they are pink. Remove from heat. Break shrimp into bite-sized pieces into a large bowl and add the cooked garlic. Remove skin, seed and chop tomatoes. Peel, seed and chop cucumber. Chop onions. Combine artichoke hearts with the other vegetables and the shrimp. Mince remaining 3 cloves garlic and combine with oil, lemon juice, herbs, and salt and pepper to taste. Beat until blended, then pour over shrimp mixture, mixing well. Halve, remove seed and skin, and dice avocado into salad mixture. Serve in small bowls with crusty French bread and butter.

Makes 6 to 8 servings

Red Bellies

These little tomato red bellies are chock-full of a delightful filling of bulgur wheat, crunchy nuts, and fresh seasonings. Spoon on the green walnut and garlic butter for the final treat.

1980 Recipe contest finalist: Bob Dixon, Santa Cruz

---

1 cup chicken stock
½ cup bulgur wheat
4 firm, large, fresh tomatoes
8 large fresh garlic cloves
½ cup chopped walnuts
3 tbsp. olive oil
¼ cup chopped fresh parsley
3 tbsp. fresh minced basil (or ½ tsp. dried)
2 tbsp. minced watercress (optional)
1 tbsp. Worcestershire sauce
Juice of 1 lemon
Salt to taste
Green Walnut and Garlic Butter

PREPARATION:

Pour heated chicken stock over bulgur. Cover and let stand 1 hour. Slice top off each tomato. Remove pulp and reserve.

Preheat oven to 350°F. Place tomatoes upside-down on paper towel to drain. Sauté garlic and walnuts in 2 tbsp. of olive oil over low heat for 2 to 3 minutes. In a medium bowl combine bulgur, walnuts, garlic, parsley, basil, watercress, Worcestershire sauce, lemon juice, salt, and reserved tomato pulp. Fill tomato shells with mixture and sprinkle with remaining olive oil. Place in an oiled dish and bake for 15 to 20 minutes. Add 1 generous tbsp. of the Green Walnut and Garlic Butter on top of each tomato and return to oven for 2 to 3 minutes.

Makes 4 servings

Green Walnut and Garlic Butter

4 cloves fresh garlic, minced and mashed
6 walnut halves, minced
1 tbsp. olive oil
½ cup butter (creamed)
4 large spinach leaves, minced
2 tbsp. minced fresh basil
Dash of Tabasco

PREPARATION:
Sauté garlic and walnuts for 2 minutes in olive oil. Mash well. Combine butter with all ingredients cover, and chill until needed.

Makes about ¾ cup

Caesar Salad California Style

In this version of Caesar salad, it is important to prepare the garlic-flavored oil several days ahead. Combine 1 cup olive oil with 1 cup sunflower oil and 7 cloves crushed, fresh garlic. Refrigerate for a few days, then strain. Now you're ready to fix the salad!

Recipe contest entry: Barbara Goldman, Granada Hills

---

1 loaf white bread, cut into small cubes
1 tsp. granulated garlic or garlic powder
Salt
12 to 14 oz. garlic-flavored oil (see recipe above)
1 clove fresh garlic
3 large heads romaine lettuce, torn into bite-sized pieces
Juice of 2 lemons
¾ cup Parmesan cheese
2 tsp. Worcestershire sauce
¾ tsp. pepper
5 eggs (at room temperature), coddled for 1½ minutes

PREPARATION:

Preheat oven to 225°F. Prepare croutons by placing cubed bread in deep roaster or baking dish. Sprinkle with granulated onion and garlic and ⅛ tsp. salt. Pour 6 oz. garlic-flavored oil over salted onions and garlic as evenly as possible. Bake for 1 hour, turning every 15 minutes, or until done. Before preparing salad, rub a large wooden salad bowl with fresh garlic. Then add lettuce and toss with 10 oz. garlic-flavored oil to coat each leaf. Add lemon juice and toss again. Add cheese, Worcestershire, and ¾ tsp. salt and pepper and 2 cups croutons. (Freeze remaining croutons for later use.) Toss salad thoroughly, but carefully. Then add eggs, toss gently, and serve immediately.

Jeanne's Low-fat Creamy Garlic Dressing

This original low-calorie recipe is equally good as a dip or dolloped on crisp hearts of lettuce.

Recipe contest entry: Jeanne Marks, Aptos

---

4 large cloves fresh garlic, pressed or minced
8 oz. plain low-fat yogurt
1 cup low-fat mayonnaise
¼ cup imitation bacon bits
½ tsp. prepared mustard

PREPARATION:
Combine all the ingredients thoroughly and serve as a dip or salad dressing.

Makes 2 cups

Garlic Green Bean Salad

A versatile, green bean dish that can be served as a side dish or combined with shredded iceberg lettuce for a delicious, crisp, and satisfying salad.

Recipe contest entry: Sylvia V. Blewener, Burbank

2 lbs. fresh green beans
4 large cloves fresh garlic
1½ tsp. salt
½ cup oil
½ cup cider vinegar
¼ cup minced green onions (use some green tops)
1 small can chopped green chile peppers

PREPARATION:

Cut beans in 2-inch lengths. Boil until tender-crisp and drain. Peel garlic and mash with salt. Add oil, vinegar, onions, and chiles. Pour over beans while hot. Toss gently. Refrigerate.

Makes 6 to 8 servings

Green Goddess Dressing

The original Green Goddess dressing was created by the chef of the Palace Hotel in San Francisco for a noted star in the days of the silent films. But without the garlic from Gilroy it would not be such a distinctive concoction! For a really new taste, top shrimp-filled papaya halves with Green Goddess dressing for lunch or a light supper.

1 (2-oz.) can anchovies
3 cups mayonnaise
¼ cup wine vinegar
1 tbsp. chives
1 tbsp. minced green onion
1 tbsp. parsley flakes
1 tbsp. tarragon leaves
¼ tsp. garlic powder
⅛ tsp. onion powder

PREPARATION:

Mash anchovies. Add remaining ingredients; mix well. Let stand 30 minutes or longer for flavors to blend. Serve with salad greens. You may toss chicken, shrimp, or crab meat with the greens.

Makes about 3½ cups

The festival was one of those happy bits of Americana when the whole town turns out.

Marjorie Rice
Copley News Service

Tart 'n Tangy Italian Dressing

It is so simple to make a truly appealing Italian salad dressing, or use as a marinade for steaks and chops.

1 cup olive oil
½ cup wine vinegar
1 tsp. instant minced onion
1 tsp. seasoned salt
¾ tsp. garlic powder
½ tsp. chives
½ tsp. parsley flakes
½ tsp. sugar
¼ tsp. dry mustard
¼ tsp. oregano
⅛ tsp. white pepper
Dash cayenne or red pepper

PREPARATION:

Combine all ingredients in a jar; cover and shake vigorously. Chill 1 hour for flavors to blend. Shake well before serving.

Makes 1½ cups

Italian Sweet-Sour Dressing

Italians are full of surprises and the sweet-sour flavor captured in this dressing is certainly different. It's especially good over crisp chunks of iceberg lettuce.

1 cup vegetable oil
⅔ cup red wine vinegar
4 tbsp. sugar
1 tsp. salt
1 tsp. celery salt
1 tsp. coarsely ground pepper
1 tsp. dry mustard
1 tsp. Worcestershire sauce
½ tsp. bottled hot pepper sauce
3 cloves fresh garlic, minced

PREPARATION:
Thoroughly combine all ingredients in a jar or blender. Refrigerate.

Makes 2 cups

Garlic French Dressing

This is a good basic French dressing with a subtle but pleasing garlic flavor. For variety, add ¾ cup crumbled Roquefort cheese, a chopped hard-boiled egg, and 3 tablespoons chopped onion.

Recipe contest entry: Barbara Van Brunt Halop, Los Angeles

2¼ cups vegetable oil
1 cup mayonnaise
¾ cup red wine or cider vinegar
8 cloves fresh garlic, pressed or minced
2 tsp. salt
1½ tsp. sugar
1½ tsp. paprika
1½ tsp. dry mustard
1½ tsp. Worcestershire sauce
¾ tsp. coarse ground pepper
¼ tsp. garlic salt
¼ tsp. onion salt
¼ tsp. celery salt
¼ tsp. seasoned salt
¼ cup catsup or chili sauce for color

PREPARATION:
Combine all ingredients and blend well. Refrigerate in a covered container approximately 24 hours before using.

Makes 4 cups

Karen's Fresh Pears with Garlic Roquefort Dressing

When the man of the house is of Danish ancestry and grows garlic and comice pears, what better combination to keep him content than Roquefort cheese and garlic dressing over the pears to make a terrific salad? This dressing is also delicious on most greens or can be used as a dip for fresh raw vegetables.

Courtesy of: Karen Christopher, Gilroy

½ cup mayonnaise
1 tbsp. cream
1 tbsp. lemon juice
2 cloves fresh garlic, pressed
1½ oz. Roquefort or blue cheese, crumbled
8 fresh comice pears
Lemon juice
8 lettuce leaves

PREPARATION:

Mix together mayonnaise, cream, and 1 tbsp. lemon juice and chill at least 2 hours. Cut pears in half and remove seeds and skins. Sprinkle with additional lemon juice to prevent browning. Place on lettuce leaves for individual servings, spoon on the dressing, and serve.

Makes 8 servings

Spicy Marinated Shrimp for a Crowd

Shrimp take a tangy bath in a spicy oil and vinegar marinade. When drained and arranged in lettuce cups with tomato and cucumber garnish, these marinated beauties make elegant, individual salads.

8 to 10 lbs. small shrimp, peeled and deveined
1½ cups dehydrated, sliced or chopped onion
1½ cups water
1 quart olive oil
1½ pints cider vinegar
1 pint capers with juice
¼ cup lemon juice
2 tbsp. Worcestershire sauce
2 tsp. salt
¾ tsp. instant granulated garlic
Few drops hot pepper sauce

PREPARATION:
Lightly sauté shrimp in a little oil or butter until just done. Reconstitute the dehydrated onion in 1½ cups of water. Alternate layers of shrimp and onions in a large flat pan. Combine remaining ingredients and pour over both shrimp and onions. Cover and refrigerate over night. Drain and serve in lettuce cups. Garnish with tomato and cucumber.

Makes about 30 servings

Rosie's Broccoli Salad

Tart and tangy garlic marinade adds zip to steamed broccoli.

Recipe contest entry: Carla Johnson, Petaluma

2 bunches broccoli
¼ cup olive oil
3 to 4 cloves fresh garlic, pressed or minced
½ tsp. salt
¼ tsp. oregano
¼ cup red wine vinegar

PREPARATION:

Cut off tough ends of broccoli and discard. Slice remaining stems and flowers into bite-sized pieces which should equal about 4 cups uncooked. Steam broccoli until just tender. Drain and cool. Toss broccoli with olive oil, garlic, salt, and oregano. Add vinegar and toss again. Refrigerate at least 1 hour to marinate before serving. Can be prepared a day ahead, and served chilled or at room temperature.

Makes 4 servings

Party-Perfect Garlic Dressing

When it's party time and you're planning a salad, try this flavorful combination. It makes a gallon of tangy dressing to perk up any fresh vegetable combination.

1 tbsp. dehydrated parsley
1 tbsp. dehydrated chives
1 tsp. instant granulated garlic
1⅓ tsp. curry powder
1⅓ tsp. dry mustard
2 tsp. cayenne
¼ cup salt
1 tbsp. white pepper
1 lemon rind, chopped
⅓ cup olive oil
1 cup white wine vinegar
2½ quarts vegetable oil
1¼ quarts cider vinegar

PREPARATION:
Moisten instant granulated garlic, parsley and chives with ¼ cup water. To this add curry, mustard, cayenne, salt, pepper and lemon rinds. While beating, first add olive oil, then vinegar. Chill well. Shake before serving.

Makes about 1 gallon

Georgette's French Dressing

This is a low-calorie, low-salt salad dressing that is great on any mixed green salad. It was named for the late Georgette Smith, home economics teacher at Gavilan Junior College in Gilroy.

Courtesy of: Louis Bonesio, Jr., Gilroy

---

1 cup low-sodium tomato juice
1 cup red wine vinegar
1 cup vegetable oil
¼ cup honey
3 to 4 cloves fresh garlic, minced
½ tsp. paprika
½ tsp. coarse pepper
¼ tsp. dry mustard
¼ tsp. curry powder

PREPARATION:

Combine all ingredients and whisk thoroughly or shake in a tightly covered jar. Add a little grated Parmesan cheese as a garnish and serve with sourdough bread.

Makes about 3 cups

Soups

An ancient Telugu (India) proverb states "Garlic is as good as ten mothers." Similarly, "Our doctor is a clove of garlic," an adage of the 17th century, implies that garlic is both healthful and helpful for treating various ailments. The idea prevails today, and mothers around the world are still prescribing old-fashioned, garlic-laced soup, especially for the common cold. While the potential medicinal value of garlic has not yet been proven, there is no doubt about the flavor benefits to be derived by the addition of garlic, a little or a lot, to almost any soup. Here you'll find wonderful recipes for everything from Gumbo to Gazpacho to Avocado, Cucumber, and Potato soups. And, of course, two first-rate versions of classic Garlic Soup.

This is no fad. Garlic is chic now—finally, Don Christopher agreed with a smile. "The future is real rosy for garlic and also for Gilroy."

Los Angeles Times

The Christophers' Garlic Soup

One of the organizers of the festival, garlic grower and shipper Don Christopher, devised this recipe for garlic soup after a trip to Mexico. He says that he made it a dozen times before he was satisfied that he had it right. Now it's one of his favorites. It's delicious when reheated too.

---

6 beef-flavored bouillon cubes
8 cups boiling water
14 large cloves fresh garlic
2 tbsp. butter
2 tbsp. minced parsley
1 tbsp. flour
¼ tsp. freshly ground pepper
6 egg yolks, beaten
6 thin slices Monterey Jack cheese
6 small slices French bread, toasted

PREPARATION:

In a large bowl or saucepan, combine bouillon cubes and water, stirring until cubes are dissolved. Peel garlic and mince (can be done quickly in a blender or food processor). In a heavy saucepan, over low heat, brown garlic lightly in butter with minced parsley, stirring constantly so as not to burn. Add flour and stir until slightly browned. Add broth and pepper; simmer at least 30 minutes to 1 hour. Just before serving, preheat broiler. Slowly add egg yolks to soup, stirring constantly. Place cheese on toasted bread and place 1 slice in each serving bowl. Ladle soup into bowl and place bowl under broiler just long enough to melt cheese. (This could also be done in the microwave oven.) Serve at once.

Makes 6 generous servings

Caulditos de Ajos *Little Soup of Garlic*

This light, fresh-tasting soup would be very satisfying served in mugs on a cold night. The combination of cilantro and lime with the garlic flavor is typically Mexican and always delicious.

Recipe contest entry: Anne Copeland MacCallum, San Pedro

¼ cup peeled and chopped fresh garlic
¼ cup oil
6 cups chicken broth
Juice of 1 lime
Salt and pepper to taste
2 eggs, beaten
grated rind of one lime
Cilantro (fresh coriander, also called Mexican parsley)

PREPARATION:

Sauté garlic in oil until golden. In a stockpot, combine chicken broth and lime juice. Add sautéed garlic, salt, and pepper and bring to a boil. Lower heat and continue to simmer for 15 to 20 minutes, or until the garlic taste permeates the soup. Meanwhile, blend eggs and grated lime rind in a bowl. Add egg mixture to garlic soup a little at a time, stirring constantly. Turn up heat slightly, but do not allow soup to boil. Continue to cook about 5 minutes. Serve with chopped cilantro and sliced limes for garnish.

Makes 6 (1-cup) servings

Italian Sausage Soup

You can make a meal of this soup by serving with a green salad, plenty of crusty French bread and... red wine, perhaps.

1 lb. Italian sausage, cut in ½-inch slices
4 cloves fresh garlic, minced
2 large onions, chopped
1 (16-oz.) can Italian pear tomatoes
1½ quarts canned beef broth or prepared from bouillon cubes and water
1½ cups red wine (or water)
½ tsp. basil
½ tsp. thyme
3 tbsp. chopped parsley
1 medium green pepper, chopped
2 medium zucchini, sliced
3 cups uncooked *farfalle* (bow-tie noodles)
Parmesan cheese, grated for garnish

PREPARATION:

In a 5-quart kettle, brown sausage over medium heat. Drain fat. Add garlic and onions; cook until limp. Stir in and break up tomatoes. Add broth, wine, basil, thyme, and parsley. Simmer uncovered for 30 minutes. Add vegetables and noodles. Cover and simmer 25 minutes more. Sprinkle each serving with Parmesan cheese.

Makes 8 to 10 servings

Bulgarian Cucumber Yogurt Soup

All over the world, Bulgarians are known for their good health and longevity, which are often attributed to the consumption of yogurt and garlic. This soup combines both in a delicious adaptation of a classic Bulgarian recipe.

Recipe contest entry: Annegret Yonkow, Fairfax

1 large cucumber
½ cup finely chopped walnuts
4 cloves fresh garlic, minced
3 tbsp. chopped parsley
2 tbsp. oil
1 tsp. dill weed
½ tsp. salt
2 cups European-style yogurt (without gelatin)
2 cups ice water
Ice

PREPARATION:

Peel cucumbers and shred or chop very fine. Mix with all other ingredients except yogurt, water, and ice. Cover and refrigerate for several hours to allow flavors to blend. At serving time, add yogurt and water and a few pieces of ice.

Makes 4 servings

Community leaders agreed that the time had come for garlic to come storming out of the closet.

Mike Dunne, *Sacramento Bee*

Cold Beet and Cucumber Soup

Even "buttermilk-haters" will like this luscious and low-calorie soup.

Recipe contest entry: Ruth Gordon, Carpinteria

1 lb. can julienne beets
1 (8-oz.) carton low-fat yogurt
1 quart buttermilk
4 large cloves fresh garlic
2 unpeeled cucumbers
4 green onions with stems
Handful fresh parsley
1 chicken bouillon cube dissolved in ½ cup water
White or black pepper to taste

PREPARATION:

Drain beets, reserving juice, and set aside in a large bowl. In a blender or food processor, combine beet juice, yogurt, buttermilk, and garlic. (Depending on work bowl capacity you may have to do this in portions.) Pour over julienne beets. In same blender, coarsely chop cucumbers, onions and parsley, using chicken bouillon for the liquid. Add to beet mixture. Stir well and add pepper to taste. Refrigerate overnight in covered container. Serve very cold.

Makes about 2 quarts

Spicy California Gumbo

If you are not familiar with Creole cookery, you may not know that the term "to rope" refers to the stringy strands which okra exudes when it first starts to cook. You may also not be familiar with filé powder which is made from the ground young leaves of dried sassafras and is used both to season and thicken soups and stews.

Recipe contest entry: Jeani Cearlock, Morgan Hill

¼ cup butter
½ lb. fresh okra
1 large onion, chopped
1½ large stalks celery, sliced
½ cup chopped green pepper
5 cloves fresh garlic, minced
2 to 3 tbsp. flour
1 jar medium-sized oysters, diced
2 cups chicken broth or bouillon
1½ large tomatoes, chopped

6 sprigs minced parsley
Pinch of thyme
Salt and pepper to taste
Tabasco sauce
Water
½ lb. diced ham
¾ lb. shrimp, shelled and deveined
Cooked rice
Filé powder

PREPARATION:

Melt butter in a large pan. Add okra, onion, celery, green pepper, and garlic and cook until okra ceases to "rope." Add flour and cook for 2 or 3 minutes. Add the liquid from the oysters, chicken broth, tomatoes, parsley, bay leaves, thyme, salt, pepper, and Tabasco. Simmer about 1 hour (may need additional water). Add ham and simmer another 20 minutes. Add shrimp and oysters and simmer for 10 to 15 minutes. Remove bay leaves. To serve, put a scoop of rice in a soup bowl and add a generous amount of gumbo; sprinkle with a little filé powder and enjoy!

Makes 6 generous servings

Avocado Bisque

Everyone likes garlic as a flavoring in guacamole. It's equally good in this elegant avocado soup.

Recipe contest entry: Mrs. John Austad, San Diego

---

2 bunches spinach, heated until just wilted but not cooked
2 medium, ripe avocados
4 to 5 cloves fresh garlic
1 cup half-and-half
1 cup chicken broth
1 tbsp. butter
1 tsp. salt

PREPARATION:

Place all ingredients in a blender and blend 45 seconds until creamy smooth. Pour into a saucepan and cover. Cook over medium heat until puffs of steam are seen at top. *Do not* allow to boil, or avocados will become bitter. Serve immediately.

Makes about 1 quart

Just mountains and cauldrons of really good, honest food.

San Francisco Chronicle

Bloody Mary Party Soup

Cocktails in a soup bowl? Why not! This spicy tomato soup is laced with vodka poured at the table from a bottle which has been frozen into a block of ice. Dramatic and lots of fun as a starter course for a brunch or light supper.

2½ cups minced onion
2 cups minced celery
1¼ cups peeled, seeded and minced cucumber
8 cloves fresh garlic, minced
2 tbsp. butter or margarine
4 (46-oz.) cans tomato juice
1½ cups lemon juice
3 tbsp. sugar
½ tsp. Tabasco sauce
½ tsp. Worcestershire sauce
1 bottle (fifth) vodka
½ cup green onion, sliced

PREPARATION:

Sauté onion, celery, cucumber, and garlic in butter until soft. Add tomato juice, lemon juice, sugar, Tabasco, and Worcestershire; simmer 7 to 8 minutes. Chill. Place vodka bottle in No. 10 can filled with water; freeze until ice is solid. Remove can but keep vodka surrounded in ice and wrapped in a towel. To serve: ladle soup into serving bowls. Garnish with green onion. Add 1 oz. jigger of vodka (from bottle in ice block) per serving of soup at the table.

Makes 24 (1-cup) servings

Great Gazpacho

The Spanish cold soup, gazpacho, is a pleasing addition to brunch or lunch and a welcome first course for dinner on hot summer days.

Recipe contest entry: Connie Rogers, Gilroy

2 medium cucumbers, peeled and coarsely chopped
5 medium tomatoes, peeled and coarsely chopped
1 large onion, coarsely chopped
1 medium green pepper, seeded and coarsely chopped
2 tsp. chopped fresh garlic
4 cups French or Italian bread, trimmed of crusts and coarsely crumbled
4 cups cold water
¼ cup red wine vinegar
4 tsp. salt
¼ cup olive oil
1 tbsp. tomato paste

Garnishes

1 cup small homemade croutons
½ cup finely chopped onions
½ cup peeled and finely chopped cucumbers
½ cup finely chopped green pepper

PREPARATION:

In a large, deep bowl combine cucumbers, tomatoes, onion, green pepper and garlic; add crumbled bread and mix together thoroughly; then stir in water, vinegar and salt. Ladle about 2 cups of the mixture at a time into a blender and blend at high speed for 1 minute, or until it is a smooth purée. Pour purée into a bowl and, with a whisk, beat in olive oil and tomato paste. Cover bowl tightly and refrigerate for at least 2 hours or until thoroughly chilled. Just before serving, stir soup lightly to recombine it.

Serve the garnishes in separate small bowls so that each diner may add his/her own according to preference.

Makes about 2 quarts (eight 1-cup servings)

Mama's Potato Soup

Don't let the homespun name of this spicy Mexican-style soup fool you. It's a great dish to serve company as well as your family.

Recipe contest entry: Edna M. Ramirez, Monterey Park

2 tbsp. oil
4 cloves fresh garlic, minced
1 cup finely chopped onion
3 medium tomatoes, peeled and chopped
½ cup chopped green chiles
1 tbsp. flour
2 quarts hot chicken broth
2½ cups peeled raw potatoes, cut into small cubes
2 tsp. salt (or to taste)
1 tsp. black pepper
2 medium carrots, peeled and thinly sliced
1 medium zucchini, thinly sliced
2 cups Monterey Jack cheese, cut into small cubes

PREPARATION:
Heat oil in a 3-quart saucepan and add garlic, onions, tomatoes, and green chiles; sauté for 3 minutes. Stir in flour and cook for 2 more minutes. Continue stirring as you pour in the hot broth. Add potatoes, salt, and pepper, cover pan and simmer over low heat for 20 minutes. Add carrots and zucchini and cook for 15 minutes longer or until potatoes are tender. Just before serving, add the cubed cheese.

Makes 4 to 6 servings

Jo's Baked Garlic Soup

"I'll never live this down," teased grandmotherly Jo Stallard as she was crowned with a tiara of fresh garlic and draped in garlic wreaths. A vegetarian, Jo has turned her cooking talents to adapting recipes for meatless cooking. This delicious soup has always been a winner with her friends, she says, and so it was too with the 1980 Great Garlic Recipe Contest and Cook-off celebrity judges.

1980 Recipe contest winner: Joe Stallard, Pacific Grove

2 cups diced fresh tomatoes
1 (15-oz.) can garbanzo beans, undrained
4 or 5 summer squash, sliced
2 large onions, sliced
½ green pepper, diced
1½ cups dry white wine
4 or 5 cloves fresh garlic, minced
1 bay leaf
2 tsp. salt
1 tsp. basil
½ tsp. paprika
1¼ cups grated Monterey Jack cheese
1 cup grated Romano cheese
1¼ cups heavy cream or whipping cream

PREPARATION:

Preheat oven to 375°F. Generously butter inside of 3-quart baking dish. Combine all ingredients except cheese and cream in dish. Cover and bake for 1 hour. Stir in cheeses and cream, lower heat to 325°F, and bake 10 to 15 minutes longer. Do now allow to boil. Mmmmm—GOOD!

Serves 4 to 6

Savory Breads, Pasta, and Pies

History recounts that the great pyramids of Egypt might not have been built without the nourishment of garlic and onions, which served as a mainstay to those who laid the cornerstones of ancient Egyptian architecture. Today garlic plays an equally important role in flavoring the many breads and pastas that are cornerstones of cuisines throughout the world. Almost everyone has a special way of preparing ever-popular garlic bread. There are a number of variations, plus some tips from experts, included in this section, as well as a garlic croissant recipe that qualified as one of the ten Garlic Recipe Contest and Cook-off finalists. For pasta lovers there are recipes using linguine, spaghetti, fettuccini, tagliarini, capellini, and vermicelli. . . and all of them *delizioso!*

Garlic Bread

Fragrant garlic bread adds crunchy delight to any meal. The main ingredients are garlic and butter or margarine, of course, but then it's the cook's choice. The garlic used might be minced or pressed or the pow-dered variety from the spice shelf. Some like to add cheese or herbs or other secret ingredients. The bread may be baked, broiled, or grilled. No matter how you like it, there's a garlic bread recipe for you. Recipes for garlic butter will be found in the Miscellaneous section of this book because they can also be used to season vegetables and other foods.

Quick Tips for Making Garlic Breads:

Take a tip from the French, who love their garlic. Rub toasted bread with a cut clove of garlic before buttering. The toast acts as a grater and leaves a layer of fresh garlic flavor on the bread.

Garlic toast can also be made by toasting bread and spreading with garlic purée or granulated garlic, then adding a sprinkle of grated breadcrumbs and olive oil before browning in the oven.

Toasted English muffins or bagels can be good substitutes for French bread. They taste great slathered with garlic butter.

For impromptu parties, keep garlic bread in the freezer. It will last for months if well wrapped. When needed, just pop into the oven still frozen.

Use baked garlic cloves to spread on hot French bread. Bake whole bulbs with the skin left on in a little oil, either in a casserole or wrapped in foil in a moderate oven until soft. The cloves will pop right out of their skins and spread like butter.

Mary's Garlic Bread

The Gilroy merchant who developed this recipe adds mayonnaise, cheese, and herbs to her garlic butter mixture to achieve a fabulous flavor.

Recipe contest entry: Mary Mozzone, Gilroy

1 cup butter, softened
1 cup grated Parmesan cheese
½ cup mayonnaise
5 cloves fresh garlic, minced or pressed
3 tbsp. chopped fresh parsley
½ tsp. oregano
1 large loaf French bread, cut lengthwise

PREPARATION:

Preheat oven to 375°F. Mix all ingredients in a bowl and spread on the bread. Wrap in foil and bake for 20 minutes. Unwrap and brown slightly under the broiler.

Makes 6 to 8 servings

Leo's Special Garlic Bread

Gourmet Alley chef Leo Goforth shares his version of garlic bread. You don't even have to mince or press fresh garlic to make Leo's specialty. Just cut cloves in half and rub over toasted French bread. It's fabulous!

Courtesy of: Leo Goforth, Gilroy

---

1 large loaf French bread, sweet or sourdough
4 large cloves garlic, peeled and cut in half
½ cup melted butter or margarine
2 tbsp. parsley, minced

PREPARATION:
Preheat broiler. Cut bread lengthwise and place on a cookie sheet under the broiler. Toast very lightly. Immediately rub cut end of garlic cloves over the surface of the bread. Brush on melted butter, sprinkle with minced parsley, and return to the oven to keep warm. Slice and arrange in a serving basket.

Makes 6 to 8 servings

Classic Garlic Bread

Here's a classic bread treatment that makes perfect garlic bread every time. Just watch it carefully to prevent burning!

Courtesy of: Karen Christopher, Gilroy

¾ cup melted butter
3 large cloves fresh garlic, minced or pressed
1 loaf fresh French bread (sweet)

PREPARATION:
Preheat broiler. Combine butter and garlic in a pan over low heat until butter melts. Do no brown! Cut bread in half lengthwise. Cut diagonal slices 2 inches wide, but not all the way through the crust. Spoon garlic butter evenly on bread. Place bread halves on cookie sheet in broiler about 9 inches from the source of heat. Broil until lightly browned. Watch carefully!

Makes 6 to 8 servings

Grilled Garlic Bread

When it's barbecue time, be sure to toss some garlic bread on the grill. Served piping hot, its zesty flavor adds a special touch to any outdoor meal.

1 loaf French bread
¾ tsp. garlic powder
½ cup softened butter or margarine

PREPARATION:
Prepare grill. Slice bread but not through the bottom crust. Add garlic powder to butter and blend thoroughly. Spread between slices and over top of bread. Wrap in aluminum foil; seal edges. Heat on back of grill 45 minutes to 1 hour, depending on temperature of coals. Serve hot.

Makes 6 to 8 servings

You could wash down the garlic sauce on garlic bread with garlic wine.

London Daily Mail

Speedy Garlic Cheese Bread

No time to cook? Here's a garlic bread recipe that's a snap to prepare, and uses garlic powder for its mouthwatering appeal.

1 loaf French bread
¾ tsp. garlic powder
½ cup butter or margarine
1 cup grated Parmesan or sharp cheese

PREPARATION:
Preheat oven to 425°F. Cut bread into 1-inch slices. In a small saucepan, heat garlic powder and butter slowly until butter is melted. Brush each slice of bread on both sides with garlic butter and place on baking sheet. Sprinkle with cheese and bake 10 minutes or until cheese melts. Serve hot.

Makes 6 to 8 servings

Bacon-Greens-and-Garlic Bread

The garlic in this fragrant bread is baked right in, so 1981 finalist Patricia Bissinger gives a warning with her recipe. "When the aroma of garlic perfumes the air you can anticipate company in the kitchen, if there is anyone else in the house, so be prepared for group participation until the last crumbs disappear."

1981 Recipe contest finalist: Patricia Bissinger, Livermore

2 packages dry yeast
1 tsp. sugar
½ cup warm water
½ cup fresh parsley
½ cup fresh basil
1½ cups buttermilk
4 pieces thick-sliced lean bacon
6 cloves fresh garlic
¼ cup bacon drippings
5 to 5½ cups unbleached flour
2½ tsp. salt
¼ tsp. black pepper, freshly ground
1 large egg, beaten
1 egg white
2 tsp. sesame seeds

PREPARATION:

Combine yeast, sugar, and warm water in a large mixing bowl. Let stand about 5 minutes until yeast is bubbly. Meanwhile, chop parsley and basil fine. Heat buttermilk just until lukewarm. Dice bacon fine and fry until crispy. Peel and mince garlic. Add to ¼ cup bacon drippings and sauté a few seconds until the aroma of garlic perfumes the air; set aside. Add 2 cups flour to the yeast mixture along with butter milk, bacon-garlic drippings mixture, parsley, basil, salt, pepper, and whole egg. Beat hard with a spoon until thick and elastic. Continue to beat in enough of the remaining flour to make a firm dough. Knead on a well-floured surface until smooth and elastic. Place in a greased bowl, turning to grease top. Cover and let rise in warm oven about 20 minutes. (To warm oven, turn oven to lowest setting for 1 minute, then turn off.) Punch down dough, divide into 2 parts and shape into 12-inch long loaves or into round loaves. Place on greased cookie sheet. Brush with egg white and sprinkle with sesame seeds. Slash top of loaves every 1½ inches. Cover and let rise until doubled, about 30 minutes. Preheat oven to 375°F. Bake for 25 to 30 minutes, until golden brown and hollow sounding when tapped on bottom. Cool on wire rack. Serve with whipped butter and a smile.

Makes 6 to 8 servings

Dilly Garlic Rolls

Buttery, herbed rolls, piping hot from the grill are easy to make when you start with the ready-to-serve variety and add your own creative touches.

¼ cup softened butter
½ tsp. dill weed
¼ tsp. garlic powder
6 ready-to-serve pull-apart rolls

PREPARATION:
Cream together butter, dill weed, and garlic powder. Pull rolls apart from the top and spread butter mixture between the sections. Wrap in aluminum foil, place on grill, and heat 10 minutes, turning over once or twice.

Makes 6 rolls

Busy Day Garlic Casserole Bread

If baking bread seems like a chore, try this easy casserole bread, rich with the flavor of garlic and oregano.

Recipe contest entry: Dorothy Pankratz, Santa Clara

1 package dry yeast
1 cup cottage cheese, heated
4 cloves fresh garlic, pressed
1 unbeaten egg
1 tbsp. oil
1 tbsp. oregano
2 tsp. sugar
1 tsp. seasoned salt
¼ tsp. baking soda
2½ cups flour

PREPARATION:

Soften yeast in ¼ cup water; in a large mixing bowl combine with cottage cheese, garlic, egg, oil, oregano, sugar, salt, and baking soda. Add flour and blend well. Let rise until dough has doubled in volume. Stir down and turn into a greased casserole. Let rise 30 minutes. Preheat oven to 350°F. Bake for 40 minutes.

Makes 6 to 8 servings

Croissants D'Ail Garlic Crescents

Barbara Spellman, a home economics teacher, became a Great Garlic Recipe Contest and Cook-off finalist with this delightful recipe. Elegant and buttery, these lovely croissants get their appealing flavor from the creamy garlic butter that is mixed into the dough.

Recipe contest finalist: Barbara Spellman, Morgan Hill

Garlic Butter

3 to 8 cloves fresh garlic
1 quart boiling water
4 tbsp. butter

PREPARATION:

Place unpeeled cloves of garlic in boiling water for 5 seconds. Drain, peel, and rinse under cold water. Bring to a boil again for 30 seconds; drain and rinse. Pound into a smooth paste in a mortar or put through a garlic press. Soften butter and mix with the garlic paste. Set aside.

Croissant Dough

4 cups flour
6 tbsp. sugar
2 tsp. salt
2 oz. yeast, softened in ½ cup warm water for about 20 minutes
1 cup water or milk (plus or minus a little)
¾ cup butter

PREPARATION:

Sift together the flour, sugar, and salt in a large mixing bowl. Add the softened yeast. Gradually add the water (milk) until the mixture forms a ball (you may need a little bit more or less liquid). Knead in the bowl or on a lightly floured pastry cloth until a smooth, elastic dough is formed. Place about ⅓ of the dough back in the bowl, and add the garlic butter to it. When this is mixed into the dough, add the remaining dough. Mix thoroughly. On a lightly floured cloth, roll the dough into a rectangle about ⅜-inch thick. Place ¾ cup butter (soft enough to spread) in the center of the dough. Bring each side up and over the butter. Seal the center and ends of the dough. Fold into thirds; turn and roll to the size of the original rectangle. Repeat this process 2 more times. Fold the dough into thirds. Allow the dough to rise at room temperature until doubled. Place on a baking sheet and refrigerate 45 minutes to 1 hour, until dough is chilled. Remove from the refrigerator and roll into a rectangle about 10 x 20 inches. Cut into 10 rectangles about 4 x 5 inches. Cut each of these rectangle diagonally. Roll each piece of dough, beginning at the wide end; curve to crescent shape; place on an ungreased baking sheet and allow to rise until doubled in size (about 2 hours). Preheat oven to 400°F. Paint loaf with egg mixed with a small amount of water and bake for 10 to 15 minutes, depending upon desired brownness.

Optional: Before rolling dough into crescent shape, sprinkle with freshly chopped parsley mixed with Parmesan cheese.

Makes 10 croissants

Golden Garlic Clouds

A quick, glorious accompaniment to roasts, steaks, and stews, Yorkshire pudding makes even the simplest of meat dishes seem extra special. The secret in the preparation is the preheating of the pans. The secret in the eating is the delicious surprise of the garlic and herbs.

1980 Recipe contest second runner-up: Jeanne Howard, Monterey Park

---

Shortening, bacon grease, or fat drippings
2 eggs
½ cup whole milk
6 or more cloves of fresh garlic or 1 tsp. garlic powder
1 tsp. dried bouquet garni, crushed
½ cup all purpose flour, unsifted
½ tsp. salt
⅛ tsp. baking powder

PREPARATION:

Preheat oven to 450°F. Be sure all ingredients are room temperature. Prepare large muffin pan (preferably cast iron) by greasing generously with either shortening, bacon grease, or fat drippings. Heat in oven until fat *spits*. Beat eggs. Add milk and mix together thoroughly. If using fresh garlic, peel and put through garlic press and add the resulting juice. If using garlic powder, sift with dry ingredients. Sift dry ingredients together, add to milk mixture and beat until thoroughly blended. Remove muffin pan from oven and quickly pour in batter to about ½ full. Immediately return to oven and bake 20 minutes *without opening oven*.

Makes about 8 large clouds

Garlic Goddess Cheese Pie

This nutritious filling nestled in a potato crust makes a rich, tempting pie that's not only healthy but soooo good!

1981 Recipe contest finalist: Jacqueline Beardsley, San Francisco

Potato Crust (see recipe below)
3 large cloves fresh garlic
1 green onion
1 lb. asparagus
15 medium-sized mushrooms
3 tbsp. butter
½ tsp. salt
½ tsp. dried basil
Dash thyme

2¼ heaping cups grated
   white Cheddar cheese
2 large eggs
¼ cup milk
Potato Crust
2 large raw potatoes
½ tsp. salt
1 large beaten egg

PREPARATION

Preheat oven to 400°F.

Potato Crust: Pare and grate potatoes. Combine with salt and turn into a colander. Let drain 10 minutes, then squeeze out excess moisture. Combine with egg. Pat into oiled 9-inch pie pan to form a crust. Bake 40 to 45 minutes.

Pie Filling: Peel and crush garlic. Trim and chop onion. Trim and chop asparagus and mushrooms. Sauté garlic and onion in butter a few minutes. Add asparagus and mushrooms along with seasonings. Cover and cook 10 minutes, stirring occasionally. Spread *half* the cheese into the baked crust, then the sautéed vegetables. Cover with remaining cheese. Beat eggs with milk and pour over the pie. Bake at 375°F, 35 to 40 minutes.

Makes 1 (9-inch) pie, 6 to 8 servings

Eggplant Pasta Fantastico

Eggplant and herbs, gently simmered, make a richly satisfying sauce for pasta. An extra sprinkling of Parmesan cheese adds zip.

Recipe contest entry: Leatrice Resnick, Los Angeles

½ cup olive oil
8 fresh garlic cloves, slivered
2 tbsp. minced onion
1 medium eggplant
1 tbsp. parsley flakes
1 tbsp. oregano flakes
1 tsp. basil
1 tsp. salt

½ tsp. ground pepper
½ to 1 cup water
Juice of ½ lemon
8 oz. spaghetti or linguine
½ cup pasta liquid
1 tbsp. grated Parmesan cheese
   plus additional cheese, if desired

PREPARATION:

In large skillet, heat olive oil. Add garlic and onion and slowly sauté until lightly browned. While garlic is cooking, peel and dice eggplant into ½-inch cubes. Add eggplant, parsley, oregano, basil, salt, and pepper to garlic mixture. Stir all ingredients well. Cover and cook over medium-low heat for 30 minutes, stirring occasionally. Add ½ cup water and lemon juice. Stir and continue cooking until eggplant is soft, adding more water as needed if mixture gets dry. (Mixture should be very moist.) Cook pasta *al dente* (just until tender; do not overcook). Drain pasta; reserve ½ cup liquid. Add pasta and liquid to eggplant mixture. Add Parmesan cheese. Toss well and heat through for 1 minute. Serve immediately with additional cheese, if desired.

Makes 2 servings

Family Favorite Linguine and Clam Sauce

This recipe, which originated in west central Italy, has been in the Robinson family for over 100 years. For variation, add 3 cups drained, canned Italian tomatoes to the sauce and simmer for 30 minutes before adding clams.

Recipe contest entry: John M. Robinson, Granada Hills

---

8 cloves fresh garlic
½ tsp. salt
½ tsp. white pepper
3 egg yolks
1 cup plus 4 tbsp. olive oil
2 tbsp. butter
3 tbsp. finely chopped shallots

3 tbsp. flour
2 to 2½ cups clam juice
3 to 4 cups coarsely chopped clams
1 cup chopped parsley
½ cup chopped basil
1 lb. linguine
Grated Romano cheese

PREPARATION:

Crush garlic in a mortar to a paste. Add salt, white pepper, and egg yolks. Whisk until lemon colored. Continue to whisk, adding olive oil a few drops at a time up to 2 tbsp. Continue to whisk, adding 1 cup olive oil in a thin stream. Set sauce aside. In a frying pan heat remaining 2 tbsp. olive oil and butter; add shallots and sauté over low heat until shallots are light golden. Add flour and continue cooking for 5 minutes, stirring constantly. Slowly add clam juice, stirring constantly, until well blended; then cook 5 to 8 minutes more, stirring occasionally. Slowly add clam sauce to garlic sauce, whisking constantly. Heat over low flame, stirring occasionally, until hot. Add clams and continue to heat through. Add parsley and basil. Heat until steaming and serve with freshly cooked linguine, prepared according to package directions. Top with grated Romano cheese.

Makes 4 servings

Garlic in the Straw and Hay

The "straw" and "hay" refer to the white and green linguine that are combined to make this colorful pasta presentation. Laced with sliced, fresh mushrooms and minced prosciutto and topped with a creamy cheese sauce, it is delightful!

Recipe contest entry: Phyllis Gaddis, Venice

---

6 tbsp. butter
8 cloves fresh garlic, minced
1 lb. fresh mushrooms, sliced thin with stems included
Dash salt (optional)
¼ lb. minced prosciutto (¼ lb. crumbled cooked bacon may be substituted)
8 oz. white linguine
8 oz. green (spinach) linguine
1 cup light cream
¼ cup chicken broth
¼ cup grated Parmesan cheese, plus additional cheese for topping

PREPARATION:

Melt half the butter in a large frying pan. Add garlic and sauté until slightly browned. Add sliced mushrooms, sprinkle with a dash of salt, and sauté for 3 minutes, tossing occasionally, or until mushrooms are lightly browned. Remove from heat. In another pan sauté prosciutto in remaining butter until browned. Remove from heat. Using two pots, prepare pasta according to package directions. The green pasta will take about 1 minute longer to cook than the white. If you drain the white pasta first, the green should be done and ready for draining when you are finished with the white. Combine both pasta in a bowl. Reheat skillet with garlic and mushrooms; add cream and chicken broth. When sauce simmers, add Parmesan cheese and stir to mix. Add both straw and hay pasta and toss to mix. Add prosciutto and toss to mix. Add prosciutto and toss again. Heat carefully, because high heat will change texture of Parmesan cheese. Just before serving, sprinkle with additional cheese.

Makes 4 servings

*Gilroy Gives Gargantuan Gastronomic
Gathering for Garlic*

San Jose Mercury

Pesto Quiche

Calling garlic "a staple of life," this Great Garlic Recipe and Cook-off finalist whipped up a classic pesto sauce and combined it with freshly laid duck eggs to create her own savory quiche.

1981 Recipe contest entry: Anahit Lemon, Berkeley

Pesto

4 cloves fresh garlic
1 cup coarsely chopped basil
¼ tsp. salt
¼ tsp. pepper, freshly ground
2 tbsp. pine nuts or walnuts
¼ cup olive oil
½ cup grated Parmesan cheese
2 tbsp. melted butter

PREPARATION:
Peel and crush garlic. Turn into blender along with basil, salt, pepper, and pine nuts or walnuts. Blend at high speed. Alternately blend in olive oil and grated Parmesan cheese. Stir in melted butter. Set aside.

Filling

1 deep dish 9-inch pie shell
4 cloves fresh garlic
1 large onion
3 tbsp. butter
3 large eggs
1 cup milk
½ cup ricotta cheese
¼ cup prepared Pesto
1½ cups grated Parmesan cheese

PREPARATION:

Preheat oven to 350°F. Prepare or purchase pie shell. Partially bake shell for 5 minutes. Peel and finely chop garlic and onion. Sauté in butter until translucent. Lightly beat eggs. Mix milk with ricotta, then combine with eggs, garlic, onion, and ¼ cup of prepared pesto. Turn into crust and sprinkle Parmesan evenly over top. Bake in top of oven at 350°F for about 4 minutes, until puffed and golden.

Makes 1 (9-inch) quiche; 6 to 8 servings

Indispensable Garlic is Lauded in Gilroy
Sunset Magazine

Country Picnic Loaf

Sourdough bread is transformed into a family-pleasing sandwich loaf. An imaginative entrée for a hot summer day, it can be prepared ahead of time and either reheated or served cold for a picnic outing.

1980 Recipe contest finalist: Jackie Howard, Morgan Hill

1 loaf round sourdough French bread
3 fresh garlic, chopped fine
1 medium-sized red onion, chopped fine
4 tbsp. olive oil
6 eggs, whipped
1 whole green pepper, coarsely chopped
1 (3-oz.) can small shrimp
¾ cup chopped leftover ham or pork
8 slices of Italian hard salami, diced
2 or 3 dashes garlic powder
1 tsp. chili powder
Dash coarse ground black pepper
6 slices Muenster or American Swiss cheese

PREPARATION:

Cut sourdough bread in half horizontally and scoop out enough bread from upper and lower sections with a sharp knife to form a dish-like loaf. (Reserve removed bread to add to a meat loaf or for making croutons.) Sprinkle bottom loaf inside with garlic and onion; then drizzle olive oil over all. Set aside. In a nonstick fry pan sprayed with nonstick vegetable shortening, sauté whipped eggs; add green pepper, then stir in shrimp, ham or pork, and salami. When the eggs are almost set, add garlic powder, chili powder, and pepper. (Add no salt as salami and spices will be adequate.) Stir until all ingredients are hot and the eggs have set. Spoon mixture over garlic and onions in bottom half of loaf, filling completely. Cover with overlapping slices of cheese and top with remaining half loaf. Wrap tightly in foil and keep warm. This can be made ahead of time and then warmed in 350°F-oven for about 30 minutes. Slice in pie-shaped wedges and serve with fresh fruit in season or a crisp green salad with a garlic, olive oil, and fresh lemon juice dressing.

Makes 6 to 8 servings

... under the pot lids of exciting ethnic cuisines garlic has sneaked back into town. The uppity little bulb is ever emerging as the prime seasoning in flavored recipes. Suddenly it's chic to reek.

Town and Country

Calzone

Choose your own filling for this type of folded-over pizza, a favorite of many tasters in the Great Garlic Recipe Contest and Cook-off audience. It can be eaten either hot or cold, and also packs well for a picnic.

1980 Recipe contest finalist: David Lehmann, Palo Alto

Pizza Dough

2 tbsp. dry yeast (2 packets)
1 tsp. sugar
¼ cup warm water (100°F)
4 cups warm water
⅓ cup olive oil
1 tsp. salt
1½ cups nonfat dry milk powder
12 cups unbleached white flour

PREPARATION:
Stir first 3 ingredients together in a warm 1-quart bowl in a warm kitchen. Set aside to proof.

Stir next 4 ingredients and 6 cups of the flour together in a large warm bowl. Then add the yeast mixture and slowly stir in 3 more cups of flour. Continue to add flour gradually, stirring very vigorously. When dough is too stiff to stir, dump out on a lightly floured board and knead until smooth and elastic (10 to 15 minutes) adding just enough flour to keep dough from sticking. The 12-cup estimate of flour can vary greatly. You can use half whole wheat flour, but the dough will not be as elastic. This should make about 6 lbs. of dough.

Cut into ½-lb. pieces for individual calzoni or pizzas. Form into balls, rub with olive oil, and allow to rise in a warm place on plates or a pan large enough so that they won't touch and stick together. Let rise until they double in size.

Pizza Sauce

1 bulb fresh garlic
⅓ cup olive oil
1 (29-oz.) can heavy tomato purée
1 (28-oz.) can peeled Italian tomatoes, diced, or 2 lbs. fresh peeled
  tomatoes, diced
1½ tbsp. dry whole basil
1½ tbsp. dry whole oregano
½ tsp. salt
1 tsp. crushed hot red pepper

PREPARATION:

Separate and clean garlic cloves. Slice thinly, crosswise. Place with oil in a kettle large enough to hold all the sauce. Heat gently until garlic is sizzling in the oil, but do not allow it to brown. Pour the tomato purée and the tomatoes into the kettle. Stir in basil, oregano, salt, and pepper. Simmer 15 minutes, stirring often, and allow to cool. Enough for a dozen individual calzoni or 3 to 4 large pizzas.

continued on next page

Fillings

Cheeses: whole milk
              Mozzarella
              Ricotta
              Bel paese
              Parmesan
              Romano

ham (prosciutto) or sausage, sliced thin
onions and/or mushrooms, sliced and sautéed with garlic
marinated artichoke hearts or black olives

PREPARATION:

Making Calzone: To form a calzone crust, take a ½-lb. ball of risen pizza dough and place on a floured board. Pound out flat with your hands, being careful to keep the round shape. (Use a rolling pin if you need to.) The dough should be evenly thin and as big around as a dinner plate. Spread pizza sauce over the whole dough, except for a 1-inch border around the edge. Distribute grated cheeses and other fillings on half the sauce area. Use any combination being careful not to pile too much on. Fold the other side of the dough over the fillings and seal the edges together by pressing the borders firmly with your fingers. Rub a little olive oil over the top of the calzone. Add 1 tbsp. of sauce or cheese on the very top for decoration and to denote which filling is inside.

Bake on an oiled pan or baking sheet in a 450°F-oven until crust is golden brown on all sides and bottom (8 to 18 minutes, depending on your oven). Each calzone will make a meal for someone hungry. Serve with wine or beer and a green salad. Calzoni pack well to be eaten cold on a picnic.

Makes 12 individual servings, or 3 to 4 large calzones

Linguine with White Clam Sauce

Make a meal in minutes with this linguine topped with white clam sauce. Add a tossed green salad to round out a quick dinner.

Recipe contest entry: Paul Dana, Sunnyvale

¾ cup olive oil
4 to 6 cloves fresh garlic
3 (6-oz.) cans chopped clams
¼ tsp. salt and pepper
¼ tsp. thyme
1 lb. linguine
¼ cup chopped parsley

PREPARATION:

Heat oil in a pan. Press garlic and cook until golden. Add clam juice from cans, salt, pepper, and thyme. Let simmer very slowly. Add clams. Cook linguine. Add parsley to sauce 5 minutes before linguine is cooked.

Makes 4 servings

As the local crops are harvested you can follow your nose to Garlic City, U.S.A.

Marjorie Rice
Copley News Service

Fettuccini Gloriosa

Guaranteed to please the gourmet palate, this 1981 first place winner was created when Rudy Melone was preparing calamari one evening and his wife, Gloria, came home with fresh mussels. They blended both sauces together and improvised this fabulous seafood fettuccine. Worth every minute it takes! It helps to have two cooks in the kitchen, one to prepare the mussels and the second to prepare the calamari.

1981 Recipe contest and Cook-off first place winner: Rudy Melone, Gilroy

Mussels

¾ cube butter
3 to 4 cloves fresh garlic, peeled and diced
1 medium onion or 5 to 6 shallots, diced
8 sprigs parsley, chopped fine
18 to 24 fresh mussels or clams (or combination), scrubbed clean
1 cup dry white wine

PREPARATION:
In a pan with a lid, melt butter and add garlic, onions, and parsley. When onions are translucent, add mussels. Cover and when mussels start to open, add the wine. Stir and remove from stove when mussels have opened. If any do not open they should be removed and discarded.

Calamari

⅓ cup olive oil
6 to 12 cloves fresh garlic, peeled and crushed
2 lbs. calamari, cleaned and cut into 2-inch strips
2 tbsp. oregano
1 cup dry white wine
1 lemon, halved
1 (8-oz.) can tomato sauce
2 shakes Tabasco sauce, to taste

PREPARATION:

Heat olive oil in a skillet; add garlic and cook until garlic is golden brown. Add calamari, cook about 1 minute, add oregano and then the wine. Cook about ½ minute longer, squeeze juice of both lemon halves over the mixture and, for good measure, throw in the lemon halves. Add tomato sauce and Tabasco, and simmer about 1 minute.

Fettuccine

Water
2 tsp. salt
2 tbsp. olive oil
1 lb. white or green fettuccine (preferably homemade)
Parmesan cheese

PREPARATION:

In a large pot, bring salted water to a rapid boil. Add olive oil and then the fettuccine. While fettuccine is cooking, combine the mussels and calamari to create the sauce. When the fettuccine is cooked *al dente*, strain and place on a large pasta platter. Mix with the combined sauce. Arrange the mussels around the platter, decorate with sprigs of parsley, sprinkle liberally with freshly grated Parmesan cheese, and serve.

Makes 4 to 6 servings

Spinach Pesto

This recipe may seem like heresy to the pesto purist, but by using readily available fresh spinach and parsley in this full-flavored sauce, it can be prepared and enjoyed the year-round. Like pesto, it's delicious over almost everything: pasta, mushrooms, French bread, sautéed vegetables, even liver.

1981 Recipe contest second runner-up: Penny Lockhart, Gilroy

6 cloves fresh garlic
1 bunch fresh spinach
1 cup fresh parsley leaves
⅔ cup freshly grated Parmesan cheese
½ cup walnut pieces
4 anchovy filets
1 tbsp. dried tarragon
1 tsp. dried basil
1 tsp. salt
½ tsp. pepper
¼ tsp. anise or fennel seed
1 cup olive oil

PREPARATION:

Peel and crush garlic. Wash, dry, and chop spinach. Trim and discard stems from parsley. Turn all ingredients except oil into a food processor fitted with the steel blade. Blend until mixture is smooth. With motor running, add the oil in a thin stream (as when making mayonnaise). When all oil has been added, taste and add additional seasoning as desired. Cover and refrigerate. Sauce will keep about 1 week.

Makes about 2 cups

Fettuccine Fragale

Garlic-buttered fettuccine, served with a creamy ricotta sauce, makes a superb pasta course or a hearty main dish. Louise Fragale sent in her favorite recipe all the way from West Virginia.

Courtesy of: Louise Fragale, Clarksburg, West Virginia

¾ cup soft butter or margarine
2 tbsp. parsley flakes
1 tsp. crushed basil
1 (8-oz.) carton ricotta
¼ tsp. salt
½ tsp. pepper
⅓ cup warm milk
1 lb. fettuccine, thin noodles, or spaghetti
3 cloves fresh garlic, minced
1 cup shredded or grated Romano or Parmesan cheese

PREPARATION:

Combine ¼ cup butter, parsley flakes, and basil; blend in ricotta, salt, and pepper. Stir in milk and blend well; keep warm. Cook pasta in boiling water until just tender; drain. Cook garlic in ½ cup butter for 1 to 2 minutes. Pour over pasta; toss lightly and quickly to coat well. Sprinkle with ½ cup cheese; toss again. Pile pasta onto warm serving platter, and spoon the warm ricotta sauce over; sprinkle with the remaining cheese. Garnish with additional parsley, if desired.

Makes 6 to 8 servings

Pasta con Pesto Alla Melone

The Gilroy Garlic Festival would not have happened without the inspiration, foresight, and creative mind of Dr. Rudy Melone.

In this recipe from Dr. Melone's private collection, he suggests a light, fine pasta to go with his gloriously garlicky pesto creation. A light salad with oil and vinegar dressing and a veal entrée are perfect with it. Pasta con pesto is also a versatile accompaniment with fish and poultry.

Courtesy of: Dr. Rudy Melone, President, Gavilan College
Chairman, Gilroy Garlic Festival

---

1 cup grated fresh Parmesan cheese
2 cups fresh basil leaves
½ cup melted butter
10 to 20 cloves fresh garlic
    (depending on their size and your taste)

1 tbsp. pine nuts
¾ cup olive oil
1 lb. pasta (preferably
    capellini or vermicelli)

PREPARATION:

Using a blender or food processor, grate enough Parmesan cheese to make 1 cup; add basil. Then add melted butter, followed by garlic, pine nuts, and finally the oil. Allow each added ingredient to blend smoothly with the preceding ones, and let stand at least 1 hour. Prepare pasta according to package directions. Mix pesto with pasta fresh from the boiling water. Do not add too much pesto, but allow each person to adjust the flavor to taste by adding more pesto if desired. Leftover pesto will last for quite a while if refrigerated in a plastic container, but do not freeze.

Makes 4 servings

Super Meat Sauce for Pasta

Sliced meat rolls add a new dimension to traditional pasta sauce. Use leftover sauce to make a delicious pizza.

Recipe contest entry: Beckley Hill, Malibu

1 whole round steak, sliced ¼ inch thick
12 cloves fresh garlic, peeled and minced
2 cups chopped parsley
4 tbsp. oil
3 (8-oz.) cans tomato sauce
2 tsp. sweet basil
1 tsp. oregano
1 tsp. salt
½ tsp. crushed red pepper
1 lb. spaghetti or other pasta
½ cup grated Parmesan cheese, or a mixture of Parmesan and Romano

PREPARATION:

Remove bone from steak and save. Cut steak into 4 pieces. Brush pieces with oil, and top with garlic and parsley, dividing evenly. Roll up each piece of meat and secure by wrapping with sewing thread. Heat 4 tbsp. oil in a heavy Dutch oven. Brown rolls of meat thoroughly. For added flavor, add the steak bone to the pan while meat is browning. Add remaining ingredients except pasta and cheese and cook over medium-low heat, stirring often, until tomato sauce has a slightly brown color. Cover and simmer 2 hours or until meat is very tender. Cook spaghetti according to package directions and drain. In a large, warmed serving bowl toss spaghetti with 1 cup sauce and ¼ cup cheese. Keep warm. Remove thread from meat rolls, and slice. Top the spaghetti with meat and more sauce. Pass extra cheese.

Makes 4 servings

Noodles Romanoff

Transform ordinary noodles into party fare in an instant using seasonings from your spice shelf.

1 lb. fettucine or egg noodles
1 cup cottage cheese
1 cup sour cream
1½ tsp. seasoned salt
1 tsp. instant minced onions
1 tsp. Worcestershire sauce
½ tsp. instant minced garlic
Dash cayenne or red pepper
⅓ cup grated Cheddar cheese

PREPARATION:
Preheat oven to 350°F. Cook pasta as directed on package and drain. Combine pasta with remaining ingredients except grated cheese. Transfer to a buttered 1½-quart casserole; sprinkle top with grated cheese. Bake 30 minutes or until cheese has melted.

Makes 4 servings

Pasta con Pesto Alla Pelliccione

Paul Pelliccione, one of the head chefs of Gourmet Alley, shares this fabulous recipe for pasta con pesto as it was prepared for the Garlic Festival.

Courtesy of: Paul Pelliccione, Gilroy

---

2 cups packed fresh basil leaves, washed and well drained
1½ cups grated Romano cheese, plus additional cheese, if desired
½ cup olive oil
½ cup melted butter
6 large cloves fresh garlic, crushed
1 lb. spaghetti

PREPARATION:
Place basil, 1 cup of the cheese, oil, butter, and garlic in a blender. Pulse to blend, pushing pesto down from sides of blender with rubber spatula; continue until you have a very coarse purée. Makes about 1½ cups pesto. Spoon 1 cup pesto sauce over freshly cooked spaghetti. Mix quickly with two forks. Add ½ cup cheese and mix. Serve with additional pesto sauce and cheese. Cover and refrigerate any leftover pesto up to a week, or freeze in small portions. The surface will darken when exposed to air, so stir the pesto before serving.

Makes 4 servings

Mary Ann's Fettuccine Zucchini

Zucchini, tomatoes, garlic, herbs and spices make a savory sauce for fettuccine.

Recipe contest entry: Mary Ann Rohm, Simi Valley

3 tbsp. butter or margarine
3 tbsp. olive oil
1 medium-sized sweet red onion, chopped
4 cloves fresh garlic, sliced
1 lb. zucchini, sliced
1 tbsp. parsley
¼ tsp. oregano
¼ tsp. sweet basil
¼ tsp. thyme
⅛ tsp. marjoram
⅛ tsp. coarsely ground black pepper
1 tsp. lemon juice
2 fresh tomatoes, chopped
1 lb. fettuccine
¼ cup Parmesan cheese

PREPARATION:

Melt butter or margarine with olive oil in a saucepan over medium heat. Add onion and garlic and sauté 5 minutes. Add zucchini and sauté 10 minutes. Add herbs and spices and sauté until zucchini is almost tender. Add lemon juice and tomatoes. Simmer. Cook fettuccine in salted boiling water until *al dente* and drain. Toss with zucchini mixture and top with Parmesan.

Makes 4 servings

Walnut Sauce from Garlic Country

A rich mixture of nuts, olive oil, garlic, and cheese make a uniquely crunchy topping for pasta.

Recipe contest entry: Mrs. Benarr Wilson, Gilroy

1 lb. egg tagliarini
2 cups walnut pieces
3 cloves fresh garlic
¼ cup butter
¼ cup olive oil
¼ cup grated Parmesan cheese plus additional cheese, if desired

PREPARATION:

Cook tagliarini according to package directions until *al dente*. While tagliarini is cooking, mix walnut pieces in blender with enough hot tagliarini water to make a paste. Add garlic, butter, olive oil, and Parmesan cheese; blend, adding enough hot water to form desired consistency. Pour sauce over drained tagliarini; toss until well coated and serve hot. Sprinkle with additional Parmesan cheese, if desired.

Makes 4 servings

Spaghetti Josephine

This recipe is a tribute to a lovely little Italian aunt-by-marriage who taught a North Carolina girl not to fear garlic. Aunt Jo hasn't been so well lately, and doesn't cook as often as she used to, but her style of cuisine lives on in a niece-in-law who turned to her husband one night and said, "How can I cook dinner—we're out of garlic!"

Recipe contest entry: Kathleen Kenney, Sausalito

1 medium head cauliflower, separated into florets
1 lb. spaghetti
5 cloves fresh garlic, minced
2 tbsp. olive oil
¼ cup minced parsley
½ cup butter
½ cup freshly grated Parmesan cheese plus additional cheese
Freshly ground pepper

PREPARATION:

Cook cauliflower in a large pot of boiling, salted water. When almost tender (about 10 to 12 minutes), add spaghetti and cook until spaghetti is *al dente*. While cauliflower is cooking, sauté garlic in olive oil about 1 minute. Add parsley and butter and cook over low heat until hot and bubbly. Drain spaghetti and cauliflower; add garlic butter and toss gently. Add grated cheese and toss again. Serve with additional grated cheese and freshly ground pepper.

Makes 4 servings

Gagootza

For your next party, serve with garlic toast, tossed green salad and beer or wine.

Recipe contest entry: Carl Stockdale, Pasadena

Olive oil
3 large sweet white onions, sliced into ⅛-inch thick rings
2 to 3 bulbs fresh garlic, pressed
3 bunches minced parsley (just tops)
14 medium zucchini, unpeeled, sliced ¼-inch thick
3 (7-oz.) cans green chili salsa
3 lbs. Italian sausage, hot or mild
2 lbs. spaghetti
Garlic salt
About 2½ lbs. Mozzarella cheese, grated
1 (7-oz.) can ripe pitted olives, halved
1 (8-oz.) can button mushrooms

PREPARATION:

Cover bottom of skillet with ¼-inch olive oil. Sauté onions over medium heat. Add garlic, parsley, zucchini, and salsa; stir lightly and simmer until zucchini becomes tender. In a separate skillet brown sausage and drain. Cook spaghetti 8 minutes in salted water and rinse with cool water. Grease six 8 x 10 x 2 pans with olive oil. Cover bottom of pans with ¾-inch layer of spaghetti; sprinkle lightly with garlic salt and add layer of sausage. Cover generously with zucchini mixture. Sprinkle grated cheese over top to thickness desired. Garnish with olives and mushrooms. Preheat oven to 350°F. Bake 30 minutes and serve immediately, or freeze without baking for future use. When ready to use, remove from freezer and bake 45 minutes at 350°F.

Makes approx. 36 servings (6 per pan)

Meats

As early as 600 B.C., the Chinese were seasoning their sacrificial lambs with garlic to make them more acceptable to the gods. The tradition of garlic with lamb carries forth to this day. But garlic enhances not only lamb; it combines well with beef, pork, veal, and nearly all other meats. Its flavor and aroma are a tribute not only to the gods, but to your dinner guests as well.

Hungarian Salami

"I'm a garlic fiend," says Amber Burney. "I'm very sure I use 10 heads a month—not cloves, heads." This scrumptious salami contains eight fresh garlic cloves and when chilled, resembles a firm pâté. Delicious!

1981 Recipe contest first runner-up: Amber Burney, Ventura

---

8 cloves fresh garlic, minced
2 lb. ground beef
1 tbsp. Hungarian paprika
1 tbsp. salt
1 tbsp. coarsely ground black pepper
1 tbsp. onion powder
1 tbsp. dill weed
1 tbsp. chopped fresh basil (or 1 tsp. dry)
1 tsp. liquid smoke
1 tsp. whole coriander seed
1 tsp. whole pickling spice
1 tsp. mustard seed

PREPARATION:
Combine all ingredients and mix well. Shape into 2 logs, each about 10 inches long. Cover and refrigerate overnight. Uncover, place on broiling pan and bake in a very slow oven, 225°F., for 2 hours. Cool before slicing.

Makes 2 salami logs

Steak and Mushrooms San Juan

A less expensive cut of meat can be tender and delicious if prepared properly. This recipe for round steak capitalizes on the tenderizing effect of wine and is a superb dish to serve over rice or noodles.

Courtesy of: Betty Angelino, Gilroy

2 lbs. top round steak, but into 2-inch strips
½ cup flour
Salt and pepper to taste
3 tbsp. olive oil
3 cloves fresh garlic, minced
2 tsp. oregano
1 tsp. rosemary
1 tsp. garlic salt
½ tsp. onion powder
½ tsp. thyme
1 cup water
½ cup red wine
1 cup sliced fresh mushrooms

PREPARATION:
Preheat electric fry pan to 420°F. Roll steak strips in flour, salt, and pepper. Add olive oil to fry pan; brown meat on both sides. Reduce heat to 220°F; add herbs and ½ cup water and steam for 20 minutes. Add remaining water, wine, and mushrooms and cook 20 minutes more, or until tender. Check periodically, adding more water if needed. Remove meat from pan. Add 1 to 2 tbsp. flour to thicken gravy, if necessary. Serve with rice.

Makes 4 servings

Flautas Al Bau

This recipe is quite easy to prepare and could serve as an appetizer or first course as well as an entrée.

Recipe contest entry: Baudelia Leaderman, San Diego

Butter as needed
1½ lbs. ground beef
½ lb. chorizo (Mexican sausage, beef or pork)
2 large yellow onions, minced
3 large semi-hot jalapeño chiles, finely diced
4 medium tomatoes, cut into 1-inch cubes
1 tbsp. paprika
Salt and pepper to taste
Juice of 1 lemon
2 tbsp. sour cream
16 corn tortillas

PREPARATION:

Melt enough butter in a large skillet to cook the beef, chorizo, onions, and chiles (chorizo should be mashed into mixture); cook until beef has browned and chorizo separates. Add tomatoes, paprika, salt, pepper, and garlic; mix together. Lower heat and let simmer about 10 minutes. Remove from heat and drain off half of the liquid. Mix in lemon juice; fold in sour cream. Let mixture stand 5 minutes to blend flavors. Divide mixture evenly into tortillas and roll rightly, using a toothpick to hold each together. Fry tortillas in broth until semi-brown. Remove and serve hot.

Makes 16 flautas

Tijuana Jail Chili

Like all border towns, Tijuana, Mexico, just across the line from San Diego, has a colorful reputation. It's hard to believe such delightful fare would be served in any of the prisons there, but regardless of how this dish got its name, it's worth preparing. Serve it with a tossed salad and plenty of cold beer.

Courtesy of: Louis Bonesio, Jr., Gilroy

⅛ lb. suet, finely chopped
3 lbs. round steak, coarsely cubed
3 cloves fresh garlic, minced
6 tbsp. chili powder
1 tbsp. ground oregano
1 tbsp. crushed cumin seed
1 tbsp. salt
½ to 1 tbsp. cayenne
1 tsp. Tabasco sauce
1½ quarts water
½ cup white cornmeal

PREPARATION:

In a Dutch oven, fry suet until crisp. Add steak cubes and brown. Add seasonings and water and bring to a boil. Cover and simmer 1½ hours. Skim off fat. Stir in cornmeal and continue to simmer, uncovered for 30 minutes, stirring occasionally. Serve in bowls with either beans and tortillas or cornbread.

Makes 6 to 8 servings

Gilroy Chili

When this recipe was served at a Gilroy barbecue to accompany grilled steaks, everyone declared it outstanding and many had second and third helpings.

Recipe contest entry: David B. Swope, Redondo Beach

---

3 cloves fresh garlic, minced
2 large onions, finely chopped
2 tbsp. olive oil
2 lbs. ground beef
1 (4-oz.) can green chiles
1 cup canned stewed tomatoes
2 cups beef stock
1 tbsp. chili powder
1 tbsp. ground cumin
1 tsp. salt
¼ tsp. pepper

PREPARATION:
In a large skillet over low heat, slowly brown garlic and onions in olive oil; stir and cook until tender. Heat skillet to hot, add beef, and cook until done. Add all other ingredients. Cover and reduce heat. Cook about 45 minutes more. Either remove grease or add a small amount of cornstarch to absorb it.

Makes 4 to 6 servings

Tamale Party Pie

This recipe comes together easily and will serve about 20 people. If you have some left over, freeze it for use another time or in individual portions for family members to prepare on the cook's night out!

Courtesy of: Florence Sillano, Gilroy

1 (1-lb.) can creamed corn
2 (8-oz.) cans hot sauce
2 large onions, finely chopped
1 cup salad oil
2 tbsp. chili powder
4 cloves fresh garlic, minced
2 cups polenta (cornmeal)
1 pint milk
3 eggs, beaten
1 can pitted ripe olives, including juice
Salt and pepper to taste
1½ lbs. lean ground beef

PREPARATION:
Preheat oven to 350°F. Mix all ingredients together and place in a 16 x 11 x 2½ baking dish. Bake ½ hour at 350°F. Reduce heat to 300°F and continue to bake 45 minutes longer.

Makes 20 servings

Green Garlic Chili

Much like Chile Verde, this recipe for Green Garlic Chili is easy and delicious!

Recipe contest entry: Wesley L. Minor, Seal Beach

2 lbs. beef (use any desired cut) cut into ½-inch cubes
½ cup olive oil
3 bulbs fresh garlic
6 fresh green chiles
½ tsp. salt
½ tsp. white pepper
1 large onion
3 large green tomatoes, diced

PREPARATION:

Heat oil in a skillet and cook beef until well done and tender. Separate garlic bulbs into cloves and peel. Place whole cloves in skillet and cook until tender. Add green chiles and onions. Add green tomatoes. Add the remainder of the seasonings and cook, covered, to retain as much juice as possible.

Makes 8 to 10 servings

Tripe à la Louis

If you haven't tried tripe, here's a recipe to give you inspiration. Simmered with tomatoes, white wine, beef stock, vegetables, garlic and spices, this dish will make your kitchen smell heavenly as it cooks. A little chopped cilantro and oregano are pleasing garnishes.

Courtesy of: Louis Bonesio, Jr., Gilroy

---

3 lbs. honeycomb tripe
3 tbsp. olive oil
1 large onion, sliced
2 large carrots, sliced
1 large bell pepper, cut into ¾-inch pieces
½ cup tomato purée
1 cup chopped stewed tomatoes
2 cups dry white wine
1 cup beef stock or bouillon

1 bay leaf
4 cloves fresh garlic, crushed
4 to 6 dashes Tabasco sauce
½ tsp. fine black pepper
¼ tsp. thyme
1 (1-lb.) can hominy
Fresh cilantro for garnish
Oregano for garnish

PREPARATION:

Cut tripe into 1 x 2-inch pieces and boil in lightly salted water for 15 minutes. Set aside to drain. Sauté in a heavy Dutch oven with olive oil, onion, carrots, and bell pepper for 5 to 15 minutes. Add tomato purée, stewed tomatoes, white wine, beef stock or bouillon, bay leaf, garlic, Tabasco, pepper, thyme, and hominy. Add the tripe to the Dutch oven and simmer 2½ to 3 hours. Serve with chopped cilantro and a little oregano to garnish.

Makes 6 servings

Beef Teriyaki

No garlic cookbook would be complete without a beef teriyaki recipe, because garlic is so important to the flavor of this Asian marinade. Alternate the meat with pineapple chunks for an appetizing presentation.

---

1 lb. sirloin beef, cut into bite-sized cubes
¾ cup soy sauce
¼ cup dark brown sugar, packed
2 tbsp. lemon juice
1 tsp. ground ginger
½ tsp. garlic powder
½ tsp. onion salt
Canned or fresh pineapple chunks
Bamboo skewers soaked in water for 10 minutes

PREPARATION:

Preheat broiler, prepare grill or hibachi. Place beef cubes in a bowl. Combine remaining ingredients, pour over beef cubes, cover, and let stand at room temperature 1 hour or refrigerate several hours. Thread cubes of meat onto skewers, alternating with pineapple chunks. Broil about 3 inches from heat 10 to 12 minutes, turning once, or cook over grill or hibachi. Serve hot as an appetizer or with rice as a main course.

Makes 2 to 4 servings as an entrée

Sherried Oxtails

On a cold, rainy night, this stew will offer warming comfort. The meat is simmered with vegetables to tender perfection in a thick, bubbling broth.

Courtesy of: Louis Bonesio, Jr., Gilroy

¼ cup flour
3 tsp. paprika
1 tsp. salt
4 lbs. oxtails, cut into pieces
¼ cup butter or margarine
2 cups boiling water
½ lb. sliced mushrooms

1 red pepper, seeded and thinly sliced
2 large onions, thinly sliced
3 cloves fresh garlic, crushed
2 beef bouillon cubes
2 vegetable bouillon cubes
2 tsp. curry powder
1 cup dry sherry or tomato juice

PREPARATION:

Blend flour, paprika, and salt. Coat oxtails with this mixture and reserve remaining flour. In a large frying pan with lid, melt butter. Brown floured oxtails in melted butter on all sides. Add boiling water; cover and simmer about 1 hour. Stir in mushrooms, red pepper, onions, garlic, beef and vegetable bouillon cubes, and curry powder. Cover and continue cooking about 2 hours longer, or until meat is very tender. Blend in sherry or tomato juice and simmer uncovered about 15 minutes longer. In a small bowl, gradually stir a little of the cooking liquid into reserved seasoned flour to form a smooth paste; blend flour paste into oxtails and cook, stirring constantly, until thickened and bubbling.

Makes 4 to 6 servings

Limas and Sausage Italiano

Spicy sausage and herbs blend well with lima beans to make a low cost and very appealing casserole.

---

1 lb. bulk Italian (or other spicy) sausage
¼ cup chopped onion
½ tsp. garlic powder
½ tsp. rosemary leaves
¼ tsp. thyme leaves
1 (8-oz.) can tomato sauce
2 (1-lb.) cans lima beans
1 cup dry breadcrumbs
1 tbsp. parsley flakes

PREPARATION:

Preheat oven to 350°F. Crumble sausage; add onion and garlic powder. Sauté in a skillet until sausage is browned, stirring and breaking up with a fork while cooking. Crush rosemary leaves and add to sausage, along with thyme leaves and tomato sauce. Drain limas; add to sausage mixture. Stir to combine. Transfer to a 1½-quart casserole. Melt butter; stir into breadcrumbs and parsley flakes, tossing lightly. Spoon over top of bean mixture. Bake in oven 1 hour or until crumbs are golden.

Makes 4 to 6 servings

Garlic is Gold for Gilroy

Sacramento Bee

Garlic Frittata

For brunch or a light supper, this frittata is a snap to prepare and the flavor is superb. Try serving it with steamed artichokes or a green salad and a chilled California white wine.

Recipe contest entry: Anne T. Kahn, Newark

8 eggs
½ cup milk
½ cup grated Parmesan cheese
2 tbsp. butter
4 cloves fresh garlic, minced
½ cup chopped onion
1 to 4 oz. Polish sausage or garlic sausage, chopped
4 large potatoes, shredded
4 oz. Cheddar cheese, shredded

PREPARATION:
Beat together eggs, milk, and Parmesan cheese; set aside. In a large oven-proof skillet, over medium-high heat, melt butter and sauté garlic, onion, sausage, and potatoes about 5 minutes or until tender. Reduce heat to medium. Pour egg mixture into pan and cook, without stirring, until eggs are almost set. Preheat broiler. Sprinkle Cheddar cheese over top of frittata. Let cook on top of stove for 1 more minute. Place pan under broiler about 6 inches from heat until top is bubbly and slightly browned. Cut into wedges to serve.

Makes 6 to 8 servings

Conejo à la Chilindron–Sautéed *Rabbit*

Tender rabbit, cooked the Spanish way, is an old country recipe you'll want to include in your family's cooking traditions after you taste its remarkably rich flavor.

Recipe contest entry: Fernandez-Carozzi family, San Mateo

---

2 to 3 lb. rabbit, cut into 6 to 8 pieces
Salt and freshly ground black pepper to taste
¼ cup olive oil
2 large onions, cut lengthwise in half and then into ¼-inch wide strips
1 tsp. fresh garlic, finely chopped
3 sweet red or green peppers, seeded and cut lengthwise into ¼-inch wide strips
½ cup smoked ham, finely chopped
6 tomatoes, peeled, seeded and finely chopped
6 pitted black olives, halved
6 pitted green olives, halved

PREPARATION:
Rinse rabbit pieces and pat dry with paper towels; sprinkle liberally with salt and a little pepper. In a heavy 10- to 12-inch skillet, heat oil over moderate heat until a light haze forms; sauté rabbit pieces to a rich brown; transfer to a plate. Add onions, garlic, pepper strips, and ham to remaining oil in the skillet. Cook for 8 to 10 minutes over moderate heat until vegetables are soft, but not brown, stirring frequently. Add tomatoes; raise heat and cook until most of the liquid evaporates and the mixture is sticky enough to coat the back of a spoon. Return the rabbit to the skillet, turning pieces to coat evenly with the sauce. Cover tightly and simmer over low heat for 25 to 30 minutes or until the rabbit is tender. Stir in olives, and adjust seasonings to taste.

Makes 4 servings

Garlic Festival Bell Pepper and Steak Sandwiches

Those who attended the Garlic Festival are still talking about the Pepper Beefsteak Sandwiches served in Gourmet Alley. Chef Lou Trinchero and his team of cooks served 700 pounds of top sirloin, 250 pounds of green peppers and 750 loaves of French bread. Thank goodness Lou has worked the recipe down to one that will "feed 4 generously." You'll want to have plenty because they are unbelievably delicious.

Courtesy of: Lou Trinchero, Gilroy

---

8 bell peppers, seeded and sliced in quarters
1 medium-sized onion, chopped
3 cloves fresh garlic, minced
¾ lb. top sirloin steak, barbecued or broiled to desired degree of doneness
8 French rolls, halved and basted with garlic butter
Garlic butter (see Miscellaneous, page 225)

PREPARATION:
Preheat oven to 350°F., or broiler, or prepare grill. In a skillet sauté bell peppers, onion, garlic, and salt and pepper in olive oil until tender. Brush rolls with garlic butter and heat in the oven or toast lightly under the broiler or over the barbecue. Slice steak thin; place 1 slice on bottom half of each roll. Top with pepper-garlic mixture and other half of roll.

Makes 8 sandwiches

Garlic Beef Enchiladas

Although at first glance this recipe may seem complicated, it is actually easy to prepare. The sauce and meat filling can even be made ahead and refrigerated. Reheat slightly when ready to use.

Courtesy of: Julie Gutierrez, Gilroy

Sauce

4 cloves fresh garlic, minced
3 tbsp. shortening
1 (28-oz.) can red chili sauce
3 tbsp. flour
1 (8-oz.) can tomato sauce

Filling

1 lb. ground beef chuck
2 cloves fresh garlic, minced
Salt and pepper to taste

Enchiladas

1 cup shortening
2 cloves fresh garlic, minced
1 medium onion, finely chopped
4 cups grated Cheddar cheese
2 (6-oz.) cans medium pitted ripe olives
2 dozen fresh corn tortillas

TO PREPARE SAUCE:

In a large saucepan sauté garlic until golden in hot shortening. Add chili sauce and lower heat. In a separate bowl combine tomato sauce and flour until smooth. Pour into chili sauce mixture and stir over medium heat until slightly thickened. Set aside to cool.

TO PREPARE MEAT FILLING:

In medium skillet over low heat, sauté beef chuck with garlic, salt and pepper until beef is browned. Set aside.

TO PREPARE ENCHILADAS:

Heat shortening in a large skillet over medium-high heat. Carefully dip 1 tortilla at a time into hot shortening, frying each side for 5 seconds. Dip the fried tortilla into cooled enchilada sauce and place on a flat plate. After you have prepared 6 tortillas, fill the center of each with meat, garlic, onion, cheese, and olives (reserving some cheese and olives to sprinkle on top). Roll up tortillas.

Preheat oven to 350°F. Pour half the sauce in a large baking dish. Then arrange filled tortillas seam-side down in sauce. Repeat, 6 tortillas at a time, until all have been cooked and assembled. Pour remaining sauce over tortillas. Sprinkle with cheese and garnish with olives. Bake until cheese is melted.

Makes 2 dozen

Crusty Lamb con Ajo

Tere Gonzalez de Usablaga, whose husband is a garlic grower, shares this exquisite method of preparing lamb that brings out a robust, garlicky flavor.

Courtesy of: Tere Gonzalez Usablaga, Celaya, Mexico

3 extra-large bulbs of fresh garlic (about 6 oz.)
¼ cup minced fresh parsley
¼ cup oil
Leg of lamb (6 to 8 lbs.)

PREPARATION:
Preheat oven to 350°F. Separate garlic into cloves and remove skins. Place garlic, parsley, and oil in a blender or food processor and mix until a paste is formed. Remove excess fat from meat. Spread garlic mixture on all sides of meat. Bake uncovered for 30 minutes per pound. This garlic mixture can also be used on other cuts of meat, such as rack of lamb, pork loin roasts, prime rib of beef, etc.

Makes 8 to 10 servings

For hundreds of miles around people came to sing songs about garlic, trade recipes and boasts about its medicinal qualities, to recall again how garlic gave energy to the builders of the Pyramids and sexual drive to their pharaohs, and to consume tons of food heavily seasoned with what is known botanically as allium sativum.

New York Times

Tortilla Loaf

Gilroy's Hispanic heritage can be seen, not only in the names of streets, ranches and public buildings, but in the types of food prepared by its citizens. Dishes like this tortilla loaf, for example, utilize ingredients native to Mexico and combine them into a wonderful supper dish.

Courtesy of: Rose Emma Pelliccione, Gilroy

1 large onion, chopped
3 cloves fresh garlic, minced
¼ cup oil
1½ to 2 lbs. ground beef
2 (8-oz.) cans hot sauce
1 (10½-oz.) can beef consommé
1 (7½-oz.) can pitted ripe olives, sliced
2 tbsp. red wine vinegar
2 tbsp. chili powder
1½ cups grated sharp Cheddar cheese
12 corn tortillas

PREPARATION:

Preheat oven to 350°F. Sauté onion and garlic in oil; add ground beef and sauté until redness disappears and meat crumbles. Add remaining ingredients, except cheese and tortillas. Cook for a few minutes to blend flavors. If sauce is too thick, thin with a little water. Place tortillas, sauce and cheese in layers in a casserole or baking dish, ending with sauce on top. Bake for 45 minutes.

Makes 6 to 8 servings

Pacific Pot Roast

There is no question that garlic improves the flavor of a simple pot roast, and tomato juice enriches the gravy.

Recipe contest entry: Elaine R. Muse, San Diego

1 boneless rolled chuck roast, 3 to 5 lbs.
8 cloves fresh garlic
1½ tsp. salt
½ tsp. black pepper
Oil for browning
1½ cups water
1 large onion, chopped
Flour
Water
1 tbsp. Worcestershire sauce
¼ cup tomato juice
Salt to taste

PREPARATION:

Make 8 slits in roast at random intervals. Into each slit insert one whole garlic clove and rub roast with a mixture of salt and pepper. Lightly coat bottom of a Dutch oven with oil. Brown meat well on all sides.

Add water and onion; cover and simmer 2 hours or until tender. When roast is done, remove to platter and thicken gravy with flour mixed with water. Season gravy with Worcestershire, tomato juice, and salt. Slice roast and serve with gravy over cooked rice.

Makes 6 to 10 servings

Beef Stew Bonesio

Nearly everyone has a favorite beef stew recipe. This one produces a gravy rich with the combined flavors of wine and herbs, and is equally good with both the meat and the vegetables.

Courtesy of: Louis Bonesio, Jr., Gilroy

1½ lbs. lean beef stew meat, cut into 1½-inch cubes
3 tbsp. flour
3 tbsp. vegetable oil
½ cup dry red wine
1½ cups boiling water
2½ medium onions, sliced
3 medium carrots, cut into ½-inch slices
3 cups potatoes, peeled and cut into 1-inch cubes

½ stalk celery, sliced into ½-inch slices
3 medium cloves fresh garlic
⅛ tsp. marjoram
⅛ tsp. dry crushed oregano
⅛ tsp. ground sage
1 tsp. thyme
2 tbsp. chopped parsley
1 tsp. freshly ground pepper
½ lb. whole small mushrooms

PREPARATION:

Remove visible fat from meat. Dredge in flour, coating thoroughly; brown lightly in oil in a 4-qt. Dutch oven. Gradually add wine and enough boiling water just to cover meat. Reduce heat and simmer, covered, for 1 hour. Add onions, carrots, potatoes, celery, garlic, marjoram, oregano, sage, thyme, and parsley. Continue to simmer 30 minutes. Remove from heat and let stand 15 minutes. Skim fat off top. Add pepper and mushrooms and bring to a boil; reduce heat and simmer 10 more minutes. Garnish with additional chopped parsley.

Makes about 4 servings

Charcoal Grilled Steak

For the best flavor, most barbecue chefs recommend marinating steaks for several hours before cooking.

---

4 rib-eye steaks, cut 1-inch thick
½ cup salad oil
2 tbsp. lemon juice
1 tsp. onion salt
1 tsp. Worcestershire sauce
¾ tsp. garlic powder
½ tsp. seasoned salt
¼ tsp. black pepper

PREPARATION:

Place steaks in a shallow baking dish. Combine remaining ingredients and pour over steaks, coating all sides. Marinate several hours in refrigerator, turning once. Prepare grill. When coals are ashy in appearance, place steaks on grill and sear on both sides. Raise grill to about 5 inches from coals. Cook 15 minutes, turning once, or until desired degree of doneness is reached.

Makes 4 servings

Lena's Meatballs

The combination of pork and beef helps to keep these meatballs moist and juicy no matter how you choose to cook them.

1 lb. ground beef
½ lb. ground pork (lean)
½ cup grated Romano or Parmesan cheese
4 slices bread, soaked in water and squeezed tightly
2 eggs
5 cloves fresh garlic, minced
1 medium onion, finely chopped
1 tbsp. chopped parsley
2 tsp. salt
1 tsp. oregano
½ tsp. black pepper

PREPARATION:
Combine all ingredients and mix well. Shape into balls. These can be fried, cooked in the oven, or dropped into hot spaghetti sauce.

Makes about 4 to 6 servings

Nervously, Epstein eyed her competitors. "Omigod," she said. "These are heavy-duty garlic freaks."

Oakland Tribune

Larry's Favorite Beef in Beer

"When Larry comes to town, he always shows up with a six-pack of beer, and a juicy round steak and pleads with me to fix this dish," explains Phyllis Gaddis about her recipe contribution. "Whether or not it's my recipe or the rest of the six-pack that makes his eyes shine when I serve it, I'll never know, but he can count on my having the rest of the ingredients."

Recipe contest entry: Phyllis Gaddis, Venice

1 round steak, trimmed of fat
½ cup chopped parsley
1 bay leaf, crumbled
½ tsp. thyme
¼ tsp. celery seed
Pinch of sage
2 tbsp. vegetable oil
3 tbsp. prepared mustard
2 large onions, chopped
Salt and pepper to taste
5 cloves fresh garlic, minced
12 oz. beer
1 cup sour cream

PREPARATION:

Cut steak into 4 portions, or slice across the grain into ¼-inch slices. Mix parsley, bay leaf, thyme, celery seed, and sage together and place in a cheesecloth bag tied with string. Cut tail of string short after knotting. In a large skillet, heat oil and sauté steak portions or slices on one side, spreading mustard on the top side. Then turn and sauté mustard-topped side. Only sear the meat on high heat. Quickly add onions; stir-fry 1 minute and lower heat. Add salt and pepper to taste, then add garlic. Pour in beer slowly, and add spice bag. Return heat to simmer, cover, and reduce heat to low. Cook for 1 hour for 4-steak portion, and about 30 minutes if steak is sliced, adding additional beer if needed. When the beer has reduced considerably, about 5 minutes before the end of the cooking time, stir in sour cream, mixing well. Raise heat slightly and serve when sauce is hot. Needless to say, we serve beer with Larry's Favorite Beef, and large salad of greens, cut tomatoes, and Bermuda onions sliced very thin with a simple oil and vinegar dressing, and sesame seeds sprinkled on top.

Makes 4 servings

Veal Shanks with Garlic

Ann Epstein, Third Place Winner in the Great Garlic Recipe Contest and Cook-off used *four whole bulbs* of garlic in her recipe for veal shanks. Garlic and veal cook together in a wine sauce for about an hour or so, and when ready, the garlic is gathered in a dish and offered to guests to spread like butter on toasty bread to eat with the meat. Be sure to select a robust red wine to go with it.

Recipe contest entry: Ann Epstein, North Hollywood

---

8 hind leg veal shanks, each cut into 1-inch pieces
½ cup vegetable oil
3 large onions, thickly sliced
1 or 2 large carrots, thickly sliced
Bouquet garni
1 cup dry white wine
2 to 3 cups brown veal stock or beef or chicken broth, enough to cover the meat
Salt and pepper to taste
4 bulbs fresh garlic
Fresh chopped parsley
Bread, cut into thick slices and toasted

PREPARATION:
In a large braising pot, brown veal shanks in hot oil until golden on all sides. Remove meat. Into the hot oil, add onions, carrots, and bouquet garni and toss until soft and golden brown. Spoon off as much fat as possible. In the same pot, arrange cooked vegetables, then veal shanks, then wine. Reduce wine completely, taking care not to burn meat and vegetables. Add the veal stock or meat broth. Bring to a boil. Preheat oven to 325°F. Separate, peel, and mash garlic; add to the simmering meat. Add salt and pepper. Cover with a layer of foil the

sides of which have been turned up so that the steam will not dilute the sauce. Cover with pot lid. Bake for 1 to 1½ hours, until meat pulls easily away from the bones. There should be 1½ to 2 cups of rich, thick sauce left. If more, reduce till required amount is reached. Onions and carrots can be left in the sauce as is, removed, puréed and added back, or removed entirely. Place meat on a pretty platter. Sprinkle with parsley. Gather all mashed garlic cloves and place in a dish. Serve meat and toasted slices of bread spread with mashed garlic. Because of the lengthy cooking, the garlic loses much of its pungency and becomes very rich and buttery in texture.

Makes 4 servings

Diane's Barbecued Mexican Lamb Chops

Bathe lamb chops in this lemony marinade infused with aromatic herbs for a Mexican-style barbecue.

Recipe contest entry: Diane Truesdale, San Jose

⅓ cup Chablis
½ cup oil
¼ cup fresh lemon juice
3 large cloves fresh garlic, minced
2 tbsp. brown sugar
2 tsp. onions, minced
2 tsp. cilantro leaves
½ tsp. ground black pepper
½ tsp. salt
¼ tsp. basil
¼ tsp. rosemary
⅛ tsp. oregano
8 thick lamb chops, center cut or shoulder

PREPARATION:
Prepare grill. Combine all ingredients except lamb chops, and mix thoroughly. Pour over lamb chops, cover, and marinate overnight. Barbecue over hot coals until chops are well-browned and tender. Serve with green salad, hot steamed rice, zucchini cooked with basil and red Spanish onions, and crisp French bread.

Makes 4 servings

Good 'n Garlicky Kebabs

Grilled lamb and vegetables make a mouth-watering meal-in-one. Use this zesty marinade for your next barbecue.

¾ cup dry red wine
¼ cup olive oil
¼ cup red wine vinegar
1 onion, chopped
5 cloves fresh garlic, pressed
1 tsp. salt
1 tsp. rosemary
1 tsp. Worcestershire sauce

1 bay leaf
⅛ tsp. pepper
2 lbs. lamb, cut into 1½-inch cubes
16 mushrooms
16 cherry tomatoes
1 large green pepper, cut in 12 chunks
1 large onion, cut into 12 chunks

PREPARATION:

Prepare grill. Combine wine, oil, vinegar, onion, garlic, and seasonings. Marinate lamb overnight in this mixture. Divide lamb into 4 portions and thread on skewers. Divide vegetables into 4 portions and thread of skewers. Grill lamb 4 inches from coals about 20 to 25 minutes, turning to cook all sides. Add vegetables the last 10 to 12 minutes. Baste meat and vegetables with marinade during the cooking process.

Makes 4 servings.

To simplify preparation of marinade, combine all marinade ingredients in a food processor. The garlic can be left whole and the onion can be cut into large chunks. Pulse to process until onion has been puréed.

Makes 4 servings

Herbed Minute Steaks

Marinating in a wine and herb sauce before grilling does wonders for minute steaks, and the topping of sour cream and paprika dresses up what otherwise might be considered a plain cut of meat.

---

1 cup vegetable oil
½ cup red wine
¾ tsp. garlic powder
½ tsp. onion powder
½ tsp. celery salt
½ tsp. salt
½ tsp. oregano
½ tsp. basil
¼ tsp. black pepper
Dash nutmeg
6 minute or cube steaks
½ cup sour cream
Paprika

PREPARATION:

Combine all ingredients, except steaks, sour cream and paprika, in a glass or enameled flat pan; mix well. Add steaks and marinate 1 hour, turning several times. Remove from marinade; pan-fry in a hot skillet, or broil just until browned on each side. Top each steak with a spoon of sour cream and sprinkle with paprika.

Makes 6 servings

Roast Tenderloin San Benito

The technique of marinating this roast before cooking helps to ensure that the meat will be juicy and tender when served.

1 (4-lb.) beef tenderloin
¼ cup lemon juice
¼ cup oil
½ tsp. salt
1 tsp. coarse black pepper
1 tsp. herb seasoning
1 tsp. powdered horseradish
½ tsp. garlic powder
½ tsp. mace

PREPARATION:

Marinate roast in mixture of lemon juice and oil 30 minutes to 1 hour, turning once or twice. Remove meat from marinade. Combine seasonings and rub over meat. Roast in 450°F-oven approximately 45 minutes for rare, or until a meat thermometer registers desired degree of doneness.

Makes 6 to 8 servings

Pajaro Peppered Tenderloin

A gourmet steak, peppery, pungent, with a zesty sauce. Excellent served with wild rice and sautéed mushrooms.

6 slices beef tenderloin, cut 1-inch thick
¾ tsp. garlic salt
½ tsp. salt
Coarse black pepper
3 tbsp. butter
1 tsp. flour
½ tsp. beef flavor base
¼ cup hot water
2 tbsp. Sauterne
¼ tsp. minced green onions

PREPARATION:
Trim off most of the outside fat and slash remaining fat every inch or so to prevent curling. Season steaks with a mixture of garlic salt and salt. Sprinkle pepper generously over each side, and press down with a knife. Sauté in butter in a large skillet, about 4 minutes on each side. Remove meat to a heated serving platter. Add flour and beef flavor base to skillet, stirring to mix well; then add hot water, Sauterne, and green onions. Bring to a boil and spoon sauce over steaks. Serve immediately.

Makes 6 servings

Spit-Roasted Rolled Rib

This classic, rolled rib roast is flavored with a delicious combination of seasonings. Serve with your favorite red wine.

---

1 (4- to 5-lb.) rolled rib roast
2 tsp. seasoned salt
1 tsp. salt
¾ tsp. garlic powder
½ tsp. onion salt
½ tsp. coarse black pepper
¼ tsp. ginger
¼ tsp. dry mustard

PREPARATION:

Prepare grill. Trim off most of the outside fat from roast. Combine seasonings and rub into all surfaces of the roast. Place on spit, 5 to 6 inches from coals, and cook 1½ hours or until desired degree of doneness is reached.

Makes 6 to 8 servings

"I love garlic so I use quite a bit," says fireman Bob Dixon of Santa Cruz.... *"I see people's faces light up after I feed them. That's my reward."*

Mary Phillips, *San Jose Mercury*

Gilroy Meat-and-Potatoes Quiche

Another finalist from the Great Garlic Recipe Contest and Cook-off, this fireman gets lots of practice cooking at the firehouse. Bob claims this dish is a favorite. When you taste it you'll know why.

Recipe contest finalist: Bob Dixon, Santa Cruz

Crust

1 lb. ground beef
¾ cup breadcrumbs
1 egg
1 cloves fresh garlic, minced
2 tbsp. Worcestershire sauce
2 tbsp. chopped fresh basil
½ tsp. pepper

PREPARATION:

Preheat oven to 350°F. Combine all ingredients and press into a 9-inch pie pan. Bake for 15 minutes. Remove from oven and set aside.

Garlic may be a lot of things, but now it's cause for celebration.

Chicago Tribune

Filling

 3 cloves fresh garlic, minced
 ½ cup diced onion
 2 tbsp. oil
 3 medium potatoes, peeled, cooked, and sliced
 4 oz. Cheddar cheese, cubed
 1 (4-oz.) can green chiles, chopped
 1 tsp. salt
 ½ tsp. pepper

PREPARATION:

Sauté garlic and onion in oil for 5 minutes. Combine potatoes (reserving enough to make ½ cup mashed for topping) and cheese with garlic, onions, chiles, salt, and pepper. Mix well and spread over the beef crust.

Topping

 ½ cup potatoes, mashed with ½ cup milk
 2 oz. Cheddar cheese
 3 cloves fresh garlic, minced
 1 egg
 1 tsp. dry mustard

PREPARATION:

Preheat oven to 350°F. Combine all the above ingredients and pour over the filling. Bake for 25 to 30 minutes.

Makes 6 to 8 servings

Scaloppine Al Limone

The term *scaloppine* describes the thin slices of veal that make this dish distinctive. Here lemon is used instead of wine and can be increased if a more *picante* flavor is desired.

---

1 lb. veal cut for scaloppine
2 tbsp. flour
2 tbsp. salad oil
1 (4-oz.) can sliced mushrooms
¾ cup water
¼ cup onion, minced
2 tbsp. green pepper, chopped
1 tbsp. lemon juice
1½ tsp. seasoned salt
1 tsp. garlic powder
¼ tsp. black pepper
¼ tsp. nutmeg

PREPARATION:
Dredge veal with flour. Sauté on both sides in hot oil until well-browned. Add remaining ingredients, including liquid from mushrooms. Cover and simmer 10 minutes. Serve from platter attractively garnished with tomato wedges, potato cakes, parsley or paprika-rimmed slices of lemon.

Makes 2 to 4 servings

Annabelle's Portuguese Pork in Orange Juice

We are pleased to present two time-honored Portuguese recipes from the wife of Ralph Santos, local garlic grower and shipper. You can give port an exquisitely different flavor when you cook it Portuguese style.

Courtesy of: Annabelle Santos, Gilroy

---

1 cup Burgundy
1 cup water
¼ cup orange juice
12 cloves fresh garlic, crushed
1 tsp. ground cumin
½ tsp. cloves
½ tsp. allspice
½ tsp. cinnamon
1 tsp. salt
¼ tsp. ground pepper
Pork loin roast, 3 lbs. boneless

PREPARATION:

Mix together all ingredients except meat. Pour mixture over pork and marinate for 48 hours, then drain off liquid and reserve. Preheat oven to 450°F. Roast meat for 10 minutes, then reduce heat to 250°F and roast another hour or until meat thermometer reads 150°F. Baste with marinade during cooking.

Makes about 6 servings

*The sweet garlicky smell of success
is in Gilroy.*

San Francisco Examiner

Veal Parmigiana

Parmigiana is the Italian word for Parmesan, the cheese that comes from Parma, Italy, and has found such acceptance throughout the world because it grates and cooks better than almost any other cheese. Its flavor combines well with garlic and other seasonings in this popular dish.

Sauce

1 (6-oz.) can tomato paste
1 (6-oz.) can water
1 tbsp. butter
1 tsp. Worcestershire sauce
1 tsp. seasoned salt
½ tsp. garlic powder
½ tsp. Italian seasoning
¼ tsp. oregano

PREPARATION:
Mix all ingredients together. Cook until sauce has thickened, stirring constantly. Set aside.

Veal

2 lbs. veal cutlets
2 tsp. seasoned salt
¼ tsp. black pepper
2 eggs, beaten
1 cup fine dry breadcrumbs
½ cup olive oil
¼ cup grated Parmesan cheese
¼ lb. Mozzarella cheese

PREPARATION:

Preheat oven to 350°F. Have cutlets sliced ½-inch thick; cut into serving-sized pieces or leave whole. Add seasoned salt and pepper to eggs; beat lightly. Dip cutlets into egg mixture, then into breadcrumbs. Brown on both sides in hot oil. Place cutlets in 8 x 13 x 1¾ baking dish. Pour sauce over meat and sprinkle with Parmesan cheese. Cover, using aluminum foil if necessary, and bake 30 minutes or until tender. Remove cover and top with slices of Mozzarella cheese. Continue baking until cheese melts.

Makes 4 to 6 servings

Annabelle's Pork Marinade

Try this light, pungent marinade on your next pork roast.

3 cups water
1 cup wine vinegar
1 tbsp. salt
½ tsp. ground pepper
6 to 8 cloves fresh garlic, crushed
½ tsp. ground cumin
½ tsp. paprika
1 (3-lb.) boneless pork loin roast

PREPARATION:

Combine all of the marinade ingredients in a large bowl. Add roast, cover, and marinate overnight. Follow the instructions for roasting pork loin on page 159.

Makes about 6 servings

Adobo

Filipino cooks have a way with garlic, as demonstrated in this classic pork adobo. It's easy to prepare and has a lovely, piquant sauce.

Recipe contest entry: Jean Baliton, Gilroy

---

3 cloves fresh garlic, minced
3 lbs. pork, cut in 2-inch cubes
15 whole black peppercorns
1 bay leaf
½ cup plus 1 tbsp. vinegar
6 tbsp. soy sauce
2 tbsp. sugar

PREPARATION:
Mix all ingredients together in large pot and simmer 1 hour. Serve with rice and green vegetables.

Makes 6 to 8 servings

Ragout of Lamb

Simmer lamb with herbs and vegetable chunks for a classic stew.

2 lbs. lean lamb, cubed
1 tbsp. oil
1 cup chopped onion
1 tsp. seasoned salt
1 tsp. celery salt
1 tsp. beef flavor base
¾ tsp. instant minced garlic
½ tsp. mint flakes
½ tsp. sugar
¼ tsp. rosemary leaves
1 bay leaf
2 cups water
3 potatoes, peeled and cut in quarters
3 carrots, peeled and cut in 2-inch slices
2 tbsp. butter
2 tbsp. flour

PREPARATION:

Slowly brown lamb on all sides in oil. Add seasonings and water; gently simmer 1½ hours or until lamb is almost tender. Add potatoes and carrots. Simmer 40 minutes or until vegetables are tender. In a separate pan, melt butter; add flour and cook until flour is brown, stirring constantly. Stir into stew and cook a few minutes longer to thicken gravy slightly. Serve with noodles, dumplings, or hot biscuits.

Makes 4 to 6 servings

Curried Lamb Chops

Lamb and curry have always made good partners. Here curry and garlic add a distinctive flavor to a basting sauce for grilled lamb chops.

½ cup vegetable oil
3 tbsp. lemon juice
2 tbsp. sugar
2 tsp. curry powder
1 tsp. salt
1 tsp. instant minced onion
1 tsp. seasoned salt
¾ tsp. garlic salt
½ tsp. black pepper
8 (1-inch thick) lamb chops

PREPARATION:

Prepare grill. Combine all ingredients except lamb chops in a saucepan. Bring to a boil, then simmer 10 minutes. Arrange chops on grill 5 to 6 inches from hot coals. Sear on both sides. Continue cooking, basting frequently with the curry sauce, 30 minutes or until chops are browned and done.

Makes 4 servings

Mrs. Joseph Gubser's Barbecued Lamb

You'll be surprised at the beautiful flavor you can impart to lamb by brushing with a simple combination of garlic and red wine.

Courtesy of: Mrs. Joseph Gubser, Gilroy

---

12 to 16 cloves fresh garlic, minced
2 cups dry red wine
8 young spring lamb, steaks or chops
Salt and freshly ground pepper (optional)
Melted butter or cream

PREPARATION:

Add garlic to wine. Let mixture stand overnight. Dip or brush (do not marinate) lamb with garlic-flavored wine and allow to stand 8 to 10 hours. Prepare grill. Grill lamb chops quickly over bed of hot coals. If desired, season with salt and freshly ground pepper. Baste with melted butter or cream. The flavor is far superior if cooked over a bed of oak or other hardwood coals.

Makes 4 servings

Pork and Green Chiles

Contrast the richness of pork with a snappy green chile sauce for a delicious south-of-the-border flavor.

Recipe contest entry: Pat Maluza, Gilroy

---

1 to 2 medium onions, coarsely chopped
3 cloves fresh garlic, minced
1 lb. pork, diced
Flour, seasoned with salt and pepper
1 large or 2 small green chiles, chopped
1 (10¾-oz.) can chicken broth
1 jalapeño pepper (optional)
1 large or 2 small fresh tomatoes, chopped
1 tsp. cornstarch mixed with 2 tsp. water

PREPARATION:

Brown onions and garlic in olive oil. Set aside. Coat diced pork in seasoned flour and brown in the same oil, adding more if needed. After the pork is browned, return the onion and garlic to the pan; add the chiles and the chicken broth. (One jalapeño pepper can be chopped up and added at this time if a sharper taste is desired.) Simmer mixture, and add tomatoes 10 minutes or so before the pork is done. When pork is done, taste for seasoning; add salt if needed. Stir in cornstarch mixture and heat until sauce has thickened.

Makes 2 servings

Lamb Shanks Divine

Saucy lamb shanks are tender and tasty from long simmering in a spicy tomato sauce.

---

4 lamb shanks
2 tbsp. flour
1½ tsp. seasoned salt
½ tsp. black pepper
2 tbsp. shortening
1 (8-oz.) can tomato sauce
½ cup water
½ cup instant minced onion
2 tbsp. lemon juice
1 tsp. garlic salt
1 tsp. sage
½ tsp. oregano
½ tsp. celery salt

PREPARATION:
Roll lamb shanks in flour seasoned with seasoned salt and pepper; brown in hot shortening. Combine remaining ingredients; pour over meat. Cover and simmer gently 1½ hours or until tender.

Makes 4 servings

Wayne's Bulgogi Korean Barbecue Meat

In the Vessey household, five or six of these Korean-style marinated flank steaks, fragrant with fresh ginger and garlic, only seem to serve six to eight people. Wayne is a grower and shipper of fresh garlic and his family really knows good flavor and good food.

Courtesy of: Wayne Vessey, Hollister

1½ cups sugar
1½ cups soy sauce
½ cup sesame or vegetable oil
20 green onions, minced
20 cloves fresh garlic, crushed
10 fine slices fresh ginger, chopped
½ cup sesame seeds
3 tbsp. pepper
5 or 6 flank steaks
Hot cooked rice

PREPARATION:

Combine all ingredients except steak and rice and marinate steaks in the sauce for 6 to 8 hours (do not refrigerate). Cook over barbecue to desired doneness. Heat remaining marinade and pour over meat and rice when serving.

Makes about 4 cups of sauce

Gilroy—the town that cloves a winner.

Los Angeles Times

Mighty Good Moussaka

We all know the adage, "You Are What You Eat," which happens also to be the title of a food column written by the third-generation winery owner who devised this recipe. If, indeed, we are what we eat, then we can count on being that much better after a portion of this wonderful concoction of delectable ingredients.

Courtesy of: Louis Bonesio, Jr., Gilroy

2 medium eggplant
½ cup vegetable oil
¼ cup olive oil
1 large onion, finely chopped
3 cloves fresh garlic, minced
1 lb. lean ground beef
1 (8-oz.) can tomato sauce
1 large ripe tomato, cut in pieces
1 bay leaf
¼ tsp. Beau Monde seasoning
1 tbsp. honey
¼ tsp. dried oregano
Freshly ground black pepper
10 fresh mushrooms, trimmed and sliced
½ tsp. ground cinnamon
½ tsp. ground allspice
1 cup partially creamed cottage cheese
½ cup dry red wine
¼ cup freshly grated Romano or Parmesan cheese
2 tbsp. chopped parsley

PREPARATION:

Preheat oven to 350°F. Peel eggplant and cut into ½-inch slices. In a skillet, heat enough vegetable oil to brown eggplant quickly on both sides. Arrange half the slices in the bottom of an oiled 9 x 12 x 2 baking pan. Heat olive oil in skillet and cook onion and garlic until golden. Add meat and cook, stirring, for about 5 minutes, breaking up any lumps. In a saucepan, heat tomato sauce, fresh tomato, bay leaf, Beau Monde, honey, oregano, and pepper to taste. Cook for 10 minutes. In a separate pan, sauté mushrooms until golden brown. Add to the meat mixture and combine. Pour the chopped meat mixture over the eggplant slices. Sprinkle with cinnamon, allspice, and cottage cheese and cover with remaining eggplant slices. Pour tomato sauce mixture and wine over all and sprinkle with the grated cheese. Bake for 1 hour until top is golden. Remove from oven and sprinkle with chopped parsley.

Makes 6 servings

Poultry

In ancient times, whole birds were roasted with their cavities stuffed with garlic in a crude attempt to impart flavor and aroma. While this method met with some success, today's sophisticated cook has a wide assortment of foodstuffs with which to vary poultry dishes, and a multitude of cooking techniques to draw upon. Yet garlic still remains a favorite to complement the characteristic good flavor of chicken and other fowl. The recipes included in this section showcase the wide range of possibilities, including two elegant game bird recipes, a Forty-Clove Chicken, and a simple broiled garlic and lemon chicken.

Oven-fried Quail

Here are two tempting recipes for preparing game birds from one of the area's best known hunters—and chefs.

Courtesy of: Peter Moretti, Gilroy

12 quail
1½ cups Sauterne
4 eggs
½ cups milk
1½ cups fine dry breadcrumbs
2 tsp. salt
1 tsp. pepper
5 cloves fresh garlic, minced
⅔ cup butter or margarine

PREPARATION:

Preheat oven to 400°F. Tie legs of quail together; marinate in Sauterne overnight. Drain and dry thoroughly. In a bowl, combine eggs and milk. In a separate bowl combine breadcrumbs, salt, pepper, and garlic. Dredge quail in egg-milk mixture, then breadcrumbs, coating thoroughly. Sauté quail in butter until golden brown on all sides. Arrange quail in large shallow baking dish or roasting pan. Cover and bake 20 minutes until quail are fork-tender.

Makes 6 servings; 2 quail per person

Pheasant in a Bag

Although pheasant is a rare bird in American markets, it's simple to prepare this recipe and makes an unusual presentation.

1 (2- to 3-lb.) pheasant
Salt and pepper
1 chopped onion
4 cloves fresh garlic, minced
Butter

PREPARATION:
Preheat oven to 350°F. Rub pheasant with salt and pepper inside and out. Rub butter on the outside of pheasant and add garlic, onion, and a little butter to cavity of bird. Put bird in a brown bag and tie end. Set on a baking sheet and bake 1½ hours.

Makes 2 servings

The contest rules specified a minimum of three cloves of garlic in each recipe. "Three cloves," she snorted. "Hah! That's a laugh. I used easily 40 cloves. In the recipe I wrote a whole head, but I just kept chopping until I had a big pile." Curiously the dish was not overwhelmingly garlicky.

Harvey Steiman, *San Francisco Examiner*

Kelly's Asian Chicken

This absolutely mouth-watering chicken was unanimously selected as the First Place Winner in the Great Garlic Recipe Contest and Cook-off. It's a simple, inspired combination that takes only 20 minutes to put together. Serve with cooked Chinese noodles and then stand back and let the compliments fly!

Recipe contest winner: Kelly Greene, Mill Valley

---

1 (3½ lb.) fryer chicken, cut into pieces, or the equivalent in chicken parts of your choice
3 tbsp. peanut oil
1 bulb (not clove) fresh garlic, peeled and coarsely chopped
2 small dried hot red peppers (optional)
¾ cup distilled white vinegar
¼ cup soy sauce
3 tbsp. honey

PREPARATION:
Heat oil in a large, *heavy* skillet and brown chicken well on all sides, adding garlic and peppers toward the end. Add remaining ingredients and cook over medium-high heat until chicken is done and sauce has been reduced somewhat. This will not take long, less than 10 minutes. If you are cooking both white and dark meat, remove white meat first, so it does not dry out. Watch very carefully so that the sauce does not boil away. There should be a quantity of sauce left to serve with the chicken, and the chicken should appear slightly glazed. Serve with Chinese noodles, pasta, or rice.

Makes 4 servings

Broiled Garlic and Lemon Chicken

Just thinking about the tangy flavor of lemon combined with fresh garlic can get the juices flowing. Add a hint of oregano and you have a marinade for broiled chicken you'll want to use again and again.

Courtesy of: Karen Christopher, Gilroy

---

8 oz. lemon juice (use 3 medium lemons)
¼ cup melted butter (or half butter, half corn oil)
3 large cloves fresh garlic, crushed or minced
½ tsp. oregano
Salt and pepper to taste
2 tsp. corn oil
1 (3-lb.) fryer chicken, cut into quarters

PREPARATION:

Mix lemon juice, butter, garlic, oregano, salt and pepper. Preheat broiler and brush pan with 2 tsp. of oil. Broil chicken, skin-side down, for 25 minutes until golden brown, basting with garlic butter sauce. Keep chicken about 12 inches from the source of heat. Turn chicken pieces, skin-side up; broil 20 minutes longer, basting frequently, until chicken is fork-tender. Garnish with lemon slices and parsley if desired.

Makes 4 servings

Garlic Chicken with Artichokes and Mushrooms

A very elegant dish which draws its subtle, but delicious flavor from the sweet and rich tasting Marsala wine that is added to complete the sauce.

Recipe contest entry: Carmela M. Meely, Walnut Creek

---

8 cloves fresh garlic
¾ cup butter
6 chicken breasts, boned and pounded flat
Salt and pepper
2 tbsp. olive oil
¼ lb. mushrooms, sliced
1 (9-oz.) package frozen artichokes, cooked and drained
1 to 2 tbsp. Marsala, sherry, or other white wine
Parsley for garnish

PREPARATION:

Mince 5 cloves garlic and sauté in ½ cup melted butter in a skillet; add chicken breasts and sprinkle with salt and pepper. Brown, then remove chicken to a warm platter. Add remaining butter, olive oil, and remaining 3 cloves garlic, minced. Brown garlic and toss in mushrooms; add artichokes. Heat. Stir in lemon juice and wine. Let thicken to desired consistency. Pour over chicken; garnish with parsley. Serve with rice.

Makes 6 servings

Chicken Rosemary

The delicate taste of rosemary gives this dish its distinctive flavor, but it's the garlic that adds zest.

1 (3-lb.) chicken
1 tbsp. flour
5 tbsp. oil
2 tsp. garlic salt
1 tbsp. seasoned salt
1 tbsp. rosemary
¼ tsp. black pepper
1 tbsp. vinegar

PREPARATION:

Cut chicken into pieces and dredge in flour. Heat 2 tbsp. oil in a skillet, and brown chicken on all sides. Remove chicken from skillet. Brush 1 tbsp. oil over bottom of a shallow baking dish and place pieces of browned chicken close together in dish, skin-side down. Combine garlic salt, seasoned salt, rosemary, pepper, and remaining oil; brush over chicken. Drizzle with vinegar; cover and marinate in refrigerator several hours before baking. Preheat oven to 350°F. Bake chicken, covered, 45 minutes. Remove cover and turn chicken skin-side up; then continue baking 20 minutes or until tender.

Makes 4 servings

Forty-Clove Chicken Filice

Don't be timid. To enjoy this dish fully, pull out a hot juicy garlic clove, hold one end and squeeze it into your mouth, discarding the skin. The garlic will be surprisingly mild, tender and buttery. Ahh...!

Courtesy of: Val and Elaine Filice, Gilroy

---

1 fryer chicken, cut into pieces
40 cloves fresh garlic
½ cup dry white wine
¼ cup dry vermouth
¼ cup olive oil
4 stalks celery, cut into 1-inch pieces
1 tsp. oregano
2 tsp. dry basil
6 sprigs minced parsley
Pinch of crushed red pepper
Juice of 1 lemon (reserve rind)
Salt and pepper to taste

PREPARATION:
Preheat oven to 375°F. Place chicken pieces into a shallow baking dish, skin-side up. Sprinkle remaining ingredients evenly over chicken. Cut remaining lemon rind into pieces and arrange around chicken. Cover with foil and bake for 40 minutes. Remove foil and bake an additional 15 minutes.

Makes 4 servings

Chicken Mama's Way

Like the classic Spanish *paella* this recipe combines chicken, sausage, and seafood in a most complementary way.

Recipe contest entry: Ressie Crenshaw Watts, Porterville

½ cup olive oil or cooking oil
4 medium sweet red onions
2 (2½-lb.) fryer chickens, cut into pieces
2 cups uncooked rice
2 cups chicken broth
2 dozen clams
2 dozen shrimp
1 dozen slices Italian sausage
4 large cloves fresh garlic, mashed
1 tsp. saffron
½ cup cooking sherry
Salt and coarsely ground pepper
Pimiento strips
Grated Parmesan cheese

PREPARATION:

Heat oil in a large casserole. Add onions and chicken pieces. Sauté until chicken is lightly browned on all sides; then add rice and 1 cup of the broth. Simmer until chicken and rice are almost tender; add clams and shrimp (if fresh, leave in shells), then sausage. Combine garlic and saffron in 1 cup of broth. Strain into casserole and add sherry, salt, and pepper to taste. Place strips of pimiento and grated cheese on top. Broil 5 to 8 minutes.

Makes 4 servings

Nofri's Garlic Chicken

This crispy-skinned chicken draws its great flavor from slivers of garlic and bits of sage which are inserted into slits in the flesh before cooking. It's easy so to prepare.

Recipe contest entry: Jeanette Nofri Steinberg, Santa Monica

---

1 frying or roasting chicken, whole or cut in pieces
Whole leaf sage
5 cloves fresh garlic, coarsely chopped
Corn oil
Salt and pepper

PREPARATION:
Preheat oven to 350°F. Rinse and dry chicken. Rub entire skin surface with a clove of garlic. With a sharp knife, make small random punctures in chicken about 2 inches apart and stuff each hole with a small piece of garlic and some sage. Salt and pepper entire chicken and place in a shallow baking pan. Brush chicken with corn oil and bake for 1½ hours, basting every 20 or 30 minutes.

Makes 2 to 4 servings

Digger Dan's Chicken

From the proprietors of a Gilroy restaurant who take pride in featuring garlicky dishes on the menu, especially at festival time, comes this recipe for chicken in a garlic, tomato, and wine sauce.

Courtesy of: Sam and Judy Bozzo, Gilroy

1 (3- to 3½-lb.) fryer chicken
4 cloves fresh garlic, minced
4 tbsp. butter
4 tbsp. oil
Salt and pepper
2 cups white wine
1 lb. ripe tomatoes rubbed through a sieve (or use 1 lb. canned Italian peeled tomatoes)

PREPARATION:
Cut chicken into quarters. Sauté garlic in butter and oil in a large pan, add the chicken legs first and brown them over high heat, then brown the breast pieces. Season with salt and pepper, lower heat, and continue cooking until the chicken pieces are tender. Remove from the pan and keep hot. Scraping off bits adhering to the bottom and sides of the pan, stir in the wine and reduce over high heat. Add the puréed tomatoes, salt and pepper to taste; stir well and cook over moderate heat for about 10 minutes. Return the chicken pieces to the pan, spoon over the sauce, and cook for a few minutes longer. Serve the chicken in the sauce.

Makes 2 servings

Gin-Gar Chicken

Second Place Winner in the Great Garlic Recipe Contest and Cook-off, this recipe combines the flavors of ginger and garlic with yogurt in an unusual marinade for barbecued chicken. Delicious hot or cold.

Recipe contest finalist: Helen Headlee, South San Francisco

---

8 oz. plain yogurt
8 cloves fresh garlic
1 (1-inch square) piece ginger root
1½ tsp. chili powder
1½ tsp. salt
1 (2½-lb.) fryer chicken, cut up

PREPARATION:
Put a small amount of yogurt in blender; add garlic and ginger and purée until smooth. Remove from blender and stir in remaining yogurt; add spices and blend well. Pour over chicken and marinate in covered container overnight, 12 to 24 hours, shaking occasionally. Cook chicken over hot coals. Serve hot or cold with lemon slices.

Makes 2 servings

Nehl's Saffron Chicken

With saffron almost worth its weight in gold, it should be reserved for use on very special dishes.

---

1 large fryer chicken
Salt
4 tbsp. oil or 2 tbsp. oil plus 2 tbsp. margarine
4 cloves fresh garlic, halved
2 bay leaves
½ tsp. tarragon
¼ tsp. saffron
¼ tsp. thyme
Pinch of sage
Salt and freshly ground pepper to taste
4 to 5 ripe tomatoes, peeled and quartered
20 ripe olives or pimiento-stuffed olives
1¼ cup Sauterne
1¼ cup chicken broth

PREPARATION:

Cut up chicken and rub pieces with salt. In a large skillet, sauté chicken on all sides in oil. When brown, blend in garlic, bay leaves, tarragon, saffron, thyme, sage, and salt and pepper. Add tomatoes, olives, wine, and chicken broth. Cook slowly for about 1 hour or until chicken is tender; sauce will be rather thin. Remove pieces of garlic before serving.

Makes 2 to 4 servings

My Own Breathtaking Cacciatore

The Italian word *cacciatore* literally means "hunter," but since this dish smells so good while it's cooking, you won't have to hunt for an eager audience to sample it when it's ready.

Recipe contest entry: Mrs. Bern H. Gershick, Los Angeles

---

1 (3-lb.) chicken, cut in pieces
3 tbsp. cooking oil
1 cup sliced onions
3 cloves fresh garlic, minced
1 (1-lb.) can tomatoes
1 (8-oz.) can tomato sauce
1 tsp. salt
1 tsp. oregano
½ tsp. celery seed
¼ tsp. pepper
½ lb. shredded Mozzarella cheese

PREPARATION:

Preheat oven to 350°F. In a large skillet, brown chicken parts in hot oil. Remove chicken and drain on paper towels. Sauté onions and garlic in remaining oil in skillet until soft, but not brown. Add tomatoes, tomato sauce, salt, oregano, celery seed, and pepper. Bring to a boil, then cover and simmer 30 minutes. Place chicken and sauce in 1½-quart casserole. Cover and bake for 30 minutes, or until chicken is tender. Remove cover and sprinkle with cheese. Return to oven and bake until cheese melts. Serve with pride.

Makes 2 to 4 servings

Chicken Pizzaiola

So many wonderful Italian dishes are made with tangy tomato sauce, and they're all good so long as they have plenty of garlic for satisfying flavor.

1 (3-lb.) fryer chicken
¼ cup butter or margarine
2 tsp. seasoned salt
1 tsp. Italian seasoning
½ tsp. salt
½ tsp. garlic powder
¼ tsp. black pepper
1 cup milk
1 cup canned tomatoes
1 tbsp. flour
2 tbsp. water

PREPARATION:

Cut chicken into pieces. In a large skillet, brown on all sides in butter. Combine seasonings, milk, and tomatoes; pour over chicken. Cover and simmer 45 minutes or until chicken is tender. Remove chicken to serving dish. Blend flour and water together; add to liquid in skillet. Simmer over low heat, stirring until sauce thickens. Pour over chicken.

Makes 2 to 4 servings

Gilroy Chicken Paprika

Hungarians love garlic, especially when it's combined with sour cream and mushrooms and the spicy addition of paprika. Serve this dish with—what else? Buttered noodles!

1 (3-lb.) chicken
¼ cup flour
2 tsp. seasoned salt
1½ tsp. paprika
½ tsp. garlic powder
¼ tsp. black pepper
¼ tsp. ginger
¼ tsp. basil leaves

Dash nutmeg
2 tbsp. butter or margarine
2 tbsp. shortening
¼ cup sherry or water
2 tsp. Worcestershire sauce
1 tsp. chicken seasoned stock base
1 (4-oz.) can mushrooms
1 cup sour cream

PREPARATION:

Cut chicken into pieces; coat with mixture of flour, seasoned salt, paprika, garlic powder, pepper, ginger, basil leaves, and nutmeg. Heat butter and shortening in a heavy skillet. Brown chicken slowly. Combine sherry, Worcestershire sauce and seasoned stock base; pour over browned chicken. Add mushrooms, cover, and simmer 45 minutes or until tender. Remove chicken to serving platter. Blend sour cream with drippings in skillet; stir 2 to 3 minutes until sour cream is heated, but do not allow it to boil. Pour sauce over chicken; sprinkle with additional paprika.

Makes 4 servings

Franco-Syrian Chicken

As the name implies this recipe combines French and Syrian cookery. "Serve with French bread and cherry tomatoes" is the recommendation of the chef who created the dish.

Recipe contest entry: Charles Perry, North Hollywood

---

1 (2- to 3-lb.) fryer chicken
5 cloves fresh garlic
2 large lemons
2 tbsp. oil and clarified butter
1 cup dry white wine

¼ cup pignoli (Italian pine nuts)
1 tsp. minced parsley
1 tsp. salt
¼ tsp. pepper

PREPARATION:

Cut chicken into frying pieces (wings, legs, thighs, etc.) Press 3 large garlic cloves onto chicken and rub all over. Let stand 10 minutes. Squeeze juice of 1 lemon over chicken pieces and marinate chicken in garlic and lemon for 20 minutes, stirring once or twice. Wipe garlic off chicken and pat dry with paper towel. Reserve marinade. Fry chicken in oil over high heat, starting with drumsticks, until the meat stiffens and browns. Add wine and marinade and bring to a boil. Reduce and simmer, covered, over low heat for 25 minutes. Meanwhile brown pine nuts in 350°F-oven for about 20 minutes, or fry in a little oil or butter over very low heat, stirring constantly. When chicken is done, remove and sprinkle with parsley. Keep warm. Add juice of second lemon and 1 or 2 more pressed garlic cloves and reduce pan juices over highest heat for 5 minutes. Season with salt and pepper and add pine nuts. Serve chicken with this gravy.

Makes 2 to 4 servings

Vermouth Garlic Chicken

"With the combination of vermouth and garlic, one needn't worry about garlic odor on the breath," says this chef whose recipe has been in the family for nearly 70 years. Actually when garlic is cooked whole for several hours, as it is here, it loses its pungency and becomes sweet and nutlike in flavor.

Recipe contest entry: France D. Williams, Carlsbad

---

1 large onion, finely chopped
2 carrots, diced
2 celery stalks, diced
½ small rutabaga, diced
Large sprig fresh parsley, minced

4 chicken thighs with bone
4 chicken half-breasts, boned
½ cup safflower oil
30 cloves fresh garlic, peeled
Dry vermouth

PREPARATION:

Preheat oven to 325°F. Combine onion, carrots, celery, rutabaga, and parsley in a large bowl and mix well. Remove skin from chicken pieces and wipe with a damp cloth. In a large skillet, heat oil and brown chicken pieces on both sides. Start with thighs first as breasts take less time to brown. Drain chicken pieces on paper towels. Spread half the vegetables and half the garlic in large casserole. Arrange chicken on top and cover with remaining vegetables and garlic. Pour Vermouth over entire mixture and cover casserole. If the lid does not fit tightly, cover with foil and then the lid. Bake 2 hours without removing lid. Serve with French bread on which the garlic cloves can be spread like butter. Delicious! A chilled Chablis is a good accompaniment.

Makes 4 to 6 servings

Chicken à la Brazil

Garlic is a part of almost every cuisine and this recipe turns to Brazil for inspiration, which in turn, draws on African flavors. No matter the country, garlic and food are good companions.

Recipe contest entry: Lirian Connell, San Rafael

5 cloves fresh garlic
Salt
2 medium onions, minced
1 medium (2- to 3-lb.) chicken, cut into pieces
2 tbsp. vegetable oil
3 large peeled tomatoes, seeds removed
3 tbsp. chopped green pepper
⅛ tsp. Tabasco sauce
Ground black pepper
2 tbsp. chopped parsley
2 cups whole kernel corn, fresh or frozen

PREPARATION:

Mash 2 cloves garlic with ½ tsp. salt until salt is moist. Add half the minced onion and mix thoroughly. Brush chicken with this paste and let marinate overnight. In a frying pan, brown chicken in oil. Remove and set aside. Mince remaining 3 cloves garlic; add to frying pan and brown with remaining onion. Add chicken, cover, and cook for 10 to 15 minutes over low heat. Stir occasionally. Add tomatoes, green pepper, Tabasco, salt, and pepper to taste, and let cook for about 20 minutes. Add parsley and corn and continue cooking for 10 minutes. Serve with white rice.

Makes 2 to 4 servings

Pollo al Ajullo

No matter what language you say it in, garlic goes with chicken. The sauce is completed with sherry and thickened slightly before serving.

Recipe contest entry: The Fernandez-Carozzi family, San Mateo

2 (2- to 3-lb.) fryer chickens
1 cup olive oil
10 cloves fresh garlic, minced
1 large onion, chopped
1 tsp. cornstarch
1 cup sherry
Salt and pepper to taste

PREPARATION:
Cut cup chickens and fry in a large pan with olive oil. When chicken is cooked, remove from pan and set aside. Add garlic and onion to pan and sauté in oil; when light brown, add cornstarch and sherry. Return chicken to pan and let cook another 5 to 10 minutes. Season with salt and pepper.

Makes 4 servings

Garlic breathes new life into a town.

Washington Post

Uncle Hugo's Chicken

Uncle Hugo likes his crunchy, garlicky chicken served with corn on the cob, a tossed green salad, and sourdough French bread with garlic butter. You will, too.

Recipe contest entry: "Hugo" David Hugunin, San Jose

⅔ cup dry French breadcrumbs
⅔ cup grated Parmesan cheese
¼ cup minced parsley
½ tsp. salt
¼ tsp. pepper
3 cloves fresh garlic, minced
⅓ cup butter or margarine
1 (3-lb.) fryer chicken

PREPARATION:

Preheat oven to 350°F. Mix first five ingredients together in a 1-quart mixing bowl. Set aside. In a 1-quart saucepan heat garlic and margarine over very low heat until margarine has melted. Remove from heat. Coat chicken pieces with butter mixture, then thoroughly coat with crumb mixture. Place coated chicken on a large, ungreased cookie sheet skin-side up. Mix together any remaining crumb mixture and butter and sprinkle over chicken. Bake for 1 hour. For crispier chicken, cook an additional 15 minutes.

Makes 2 to 4 servings

Burgundy Chicken Mozzone

The rich flavor of Burgundy seems to meld all the flavors into one in this recipe which combines green peppers and mushrooms with the chicken.

Courtesy of: Mary Mozzone, Gilroy

2 (3-lb.) chickens, cut in pieces
Flour
4 tbsp. oil
1 (8-oz.) can tomato sauce
½ cup Burgundy
Salt and pepper to taste
Dash of oregano
4 cloves fresh garlic, minced
3 large bell peppers, sliced, seeds removed
1 lb. sliced mushrooms
Fresh parsley, chopped
Parmesan cheese, grated

PREPARATION:
Preheat oven to 350°F. Dredge chicken in flour and brown in oil. While chicken is browning, mix tomato sauce, wine, salt, pepper, and oregano in a small bowl. After chicken is brown, place in ovenproof baking dish. Add garlic to pan drippings and sauté ½ minute. Add peppers and mushrooms, stir-fry 5 minutes, then add sauce. Simmer 3 to 4 minutes, and pour over chicken. Cover with foil and bake for 45 minutes. Garnish with parsley and Parmesan cheese.

Makes 4 to 6 servings

Chicken in Garlic Mushroom Sauce

The wonderful, rich creamy mushroom sauce turns this garlic chicken into a special event.

Recipe contest entry: Robin Lee Perkins, Covina

¼ cup butter
2 tbsp. vegetable oil
1 (3-lb.) fryer chicken,
   cut into serving pieces
30 cloves fresh garlic, minced
1 chopped onion
1 cup dry white wine
¼ cup water

¼ cup milk
1 tsp. salt
Freshly ground pepper to taste
½ tsp. cayenne
1 lb. sliced mushrooms
3 egg yolks
1 cup heavy cream

PREPARATION:

In a Dutch oven, melt butter with oil on medium heat. Add chicken, brown well, turning occasionally. When brown, remove pieces to a bowl. In a saucepan, sauté garlic and onion until golden brown. Add wine, water, milk, salt, pepper, and cayenne. Stir to loosen browned bits and bring to a boil. Return chicken to pan and add mushrooms. Cover and cook over low heat until tender, about 45 minutes to 1 hour. Remove chicken to a warm serving plate. Cover with foil and keep warm. Beat yolks into heavy cream until well mixed. Stir into pan drippings. Cook until thickened but do not boil. Spoon some of the sauce on the chicken; offer remainder separately. Serve with rice if desired.

Makes 3 to 4 servings

Helen's Baggy Henny

"So pretty with their golden brown glaze and even better to eat. Everyone will think that you spent all day slaving over a hot oven," says Helen Headlee, two-time finalist in the Great Garlic Recipe Contest and Cook-off.

1980 Recipe contest entry: Helen Headlee, South San Francisco

---

1 (6-oz.) package long grain and wild rice mixture (or use your favorite stuffing)
2 cups water
4 to 6 Cornish game hens (one per person)
½ cup soy sauce
½ cup honey
½ tsp. paprika
1½ tsp. salt
8 cloves fresh garlic, peeled and sliced
3 slices ginger root, peeled and cut coarsely
2 cups flour
4 to 6 small brown paper bags (lunch size)
Salad oil

PREPARATION:

Cook rice using 2 cups water for 20 minutes. Allow to cool. Wash and dry hens. Cook soy sauce, honey, seasonings, garlic, and ginger together, stirring until it comes to a boil. Remove from heat.

Put flour in a large paper or plastic bag. Place hens in the bag and shake until hens are coated with flour. Roll the floured hens in the soy mixture coating each hen thoroughly.

Preheat oven to 350°F. Place small paper bags on a cookie sheet (do one at a time). Pour salad oil all over each bag, saturating it well. (This is the messy part and you'll say "Ugh," but keep on.) When all the bags are soaked with oil set them aside. Wipe excess oil off cookie sheet. Spoon the cooked rice (or stuffing) into the hen. Slip the hen into the oiled paper bag. Staple the end shut. Place the bags of hens on cookie racks on the cookie sheet. Bake for 1 hour. Split bag open. If not brown enough, return to oven for a few more minutes.

Makes 4 to 6 hens; 1 per person

Mediterranean Chicken Breasts

Here is another mouthwatering 40-clove chicken. In this version, succulent chicken breasts are marinated in seasoned lemon juice, lightly coated, and combined with blanched fresh garlic cloves that are so sweet you can eat them by the handful.

1980 Recipe contest entry: Karen Mahshi, Concord

---

2 lemons
4 large cloves garlic, minced
1½ tsp. salt
1 tsp. chopped fresh oregano
¼ tsp. freshly ground pepper
½ tsp. cup olive oil
¼ cup safflower oil
8 boneless, skinless breasts from 4 fryer chickens
1 cup freshly grated Parmesan cheese
1 cup fine, white, fresh breadcrumbs
2 cups chicken stock (canned or homemade)
30 to 40 garlic cloves, peeled
Butter
1 cup dry white wine
⅓ cup minced fresh parsley leaves
Parsley sprigs

PREPARATION:

Remove lemon zest and mince. With wide-bladed knife, make a paste of minced garlic and salt. Combine lemon zest, 2 tbsp. lemon juice, garlic paste, oregano, pepper, and oil (Alternate method: Place unminced zest and garlic cloves in a food processor and process a few seconds using steel blade. Add

198

salt, pepper, oregano leaves, and lemon juice. With processor turned on, add oils in a slow stream.) Coat chicken breasts with marinade; let stand several hours or overnight. Remove from marinade and scrape off excess. Roll chicken in mixture of Parmesan and breadcrumbs. Place coated chicken breasts on waxed paper; allow to set 15 minutes to several hours. Preheat oven to 350°F. Heat chicken stock to boiling and blanch 30 to 40 garlic cloves for 10 minutes. Remove and drain garlic. Reserve stock for sauce, reducing to 1½ cups while chicken is baking. Place chicken in a shallow baking dish, coated with butter. Drizzle a little melted butter on each breast. Strew blanched garlic cloves over and around chicken. Cover with foil and bake 15 to 20 minutes, or until nearly done. Remove foil and place chicken under broiler until golden brown. Remove to a heated platter and distribute the garlic around the chicken. Keep warm while preparing sauce. Add dry white wine to the juices remaining in the baking pan after the chicken is removed. Deglaze pan over high heat, scraping up any brown bits clinging to bottom and side. Pour mixture into sauce pan and reduce over high heat to ¼ cup. Add reserved chicken stock and minced parsley and reduce mixture to about 1 cup. Add lemon juice, salt and pepper to taste. Pour some sauce over chicken breasts and garnish platter with sprigs of parsley. Pass remaining sauce in a pitcher.

Makes 8 servings

Garlic Festival outdoes Super Bowl.

Amsterdam New York Recorder

Seafood

During the Renaissance, banquet guests were moved to compose verses saluting the versatile garlic bulb. We think you'll be composing your own odes to seafood combined with the goodness of garlic, when you sample the delectable recipes included here. Bass, trout, calamari, scampi, clams, and salmon are just a few of the fruits of the sea made worthy of a poet's praise by including garlic in their preparation.

Sweltering over huge iron skillets, Filice and his chefs dumped in squid by the carton, fresh garlic by the small shovel, fresh tomatoes by the bucket...

Mike Dunne, *Sacramento Bee*

Calamari, Festival-style

One of Gourmet Alley's greatest attractions is watching the preparation of calamari. Some argue that eating it is even better. Here is head chef Val Filice's recipe for calamari as it is served at the Festival.

Courtesy of: Val Filice, Gilroy

---

3 lbs. calamari, cleaned and cut into bite-sized pieces
⅓ cup olive oil
¼ cup white wine
¼ cup dry sherry
1 tbsp. crushed fresh garlic
½ lemon
1 tsp. dry basil or 1 tbsp. fresh
1 tsp. dry oregano or 1 tbsp. fresh
¼ tsp. dry crushed red pepper
Red Sauce

PREPARATION:
In a large skillet heat olive oil over high heat. Add wine and sherry and sauté crushed garlic. Squeeze the juice of ½ lemon into the pan and place lemon rind in pan. Sprinkle herbs over and add calamari. Sauté calamari for approximately 4 minutes on high heat. Do not overcook.

Red Sauce

1 lb. whole, peeled tomatoes, canned or fresh
1 tbsp. olive oil
½ green pepper, chopped
1 stalk celery, chopped
1 medium yellow onion, chopped
3 cloves fresh garlic, minced

PREPARATION:

Mash tomatoes with potato masher and set aside. In a medium pan heat oil, add chopped ingredients, and sauté until onion is translucent. Add mashed tomatoes and simmer for ½ hour. Pour red sauce over calamari and heat for 1 minute.

Makes 6 to 8 servings

Fame's nothing to sniff at in Gilroy.

Washington Post

Scampi in Butter Sauce

A festival favorite, Scampi in Butter Sauce is another Gourmet Alley delicacy. The recipe here is courtesy of Val Filice who has served this exceptional dish to the delight of friends and family for years. Scampi, by the way, are close relatives of shrimp but have no exact equivalent outside Italian waters. Substitute prawns or shrimp of medium to large size.

Courtesy of: Val Filice, Gilroy

Butter Sauce

½ to 1 cup butter
1 tbsp. finely minced fresh garlic
8 oz. clam juice
¼ cup flour
⅓ cup white wine
juice of ½ lemon
1 tbsp. fresh minced parsley
1 tsp. dry basil
¼ tsp. nutmeg
Salt and pepper to taste
½ cup half-and-half

PREPARATION:

Melt butter with garlic in a small saucepan over medium heat; do not let butter brown. In a separate bowl, mix clam juice, parsley, and flour, blending until mixture is smooth. Pour flour mixture into garlic butter and stir until smooth and well blended. Stir in wine, lemon juice, herbs, and spices, stirring constantly. Gradually add half-and-half and stir until thickened. Simmer for ½ hour to 45 minutes.

Scampi

2 tbsp. butter
⅓ cup olive oil
1 tbsp. minced fresh garlic
Juice of 1 lemon (reserve rind)
1 tbsp. fresh chopped parsley or 1 tsp. dry
½ tsp. crushed red pepper
1 tbsp. fresh basil or 1 tsp. dry
¼ cup white wine
Dash of dry vermouth
Salt and pepper to taste
3 lbs. scampi (or prawns), deveined and cleaned

PREPARATION:

Melt butter in large saucepan over high heat and add oil. Combine remaining ingredients, keeping scampi aside until last minute. Add scampi and sauté until firm and slightly pink. Do not overcook. Pour 1 cup of butter sauce over scampi. Refrigerate the rest for later use.

Makes 6 to 8 servings

Garlic-laced specialties were prepared in giant pans from morning to night as wave after wave of festival goers followed their noses to the bustling outdoor kitchen area.

Vacaville Reporter

Bass and Swiss Chard

Long a favorite with Europeans, chard is becoming more popular in this country as people begin to appreciate the need to include more dark, leafy greens in their diet. The chard in this recipe helps to keep the fish moist and benefits from the taste imparted by the other ingredients.

Courtesy of: Emma Morretti, Gilroy

2 tbsp. olive oil
1 whole bass, about 4 lbs.
Salt and pepper to taste
2 large bunches Swiss chard
4 cloves fresh garlic, minced
2 medium onions, chopped
2 (1 lb. each) cans solid pack tomatoes

PREPARATION:
Preheat oven to 350°F. In a large covered roasting pan or casserole, place oil and then bass; sprinkle with salt and pepper. Cut chard into 3-inch pieces and lay on top of bass with garlic and onion. Pour tomatoes on top. Bake for 1½ hours, covered. Remove cover and bake another ½ hour. Serve immediately from the baking dish.

Makes 4 to 6 servings

Garlic's time has come...

Washington Post

Succulent Sautéed Shrimp

Garlic is the perfect seasoning to use with shrimp. Try this fast, easy recipe and serve on a bed of white rice.

---

1 lb. uncooked shrimp
¼ cup butter
2 tbsp. lemon juice
1 tsp. parsley flakes
1 tsp. chives
¾ tsp. seasoned salt
½ tsp. garlic powder
½ tsp. dry mustard
½ tsp. tarragon leaves
⅛ tsp. cayenne or red pepper

PREPARATION:

Shell and devein shrimp. Melt butter in a chafing dish or skillet; add lemon juice and seasonings. Sauté shrimp in hot herb butter over medium heat 8 minutes or until pink, turning once. Serve hot.

Makes 2 or 3 servings

Insalata di Calamari

The Italians like their calamari deep fried, in seafood stews, in sauces for pasta, and in many other popular dishes. It is also absolutely delicious served cold as a tangy fresh salad. This recipe could also be served in small portions as an appetizer.

Courtesy of: John Filice, Aptos

5 lbs. calamari, cleaned (bodies cut into rings and tentacles separated)
¼ cup olive oil
1 medium bunch parsley, chopped
5 (4-oz.) jars whole pimientos
½ cup olive oil
5 to 10 cloves fresh garlic
1 to 2 (2-oz.) cans anchovies
Worcestershire sauce
1 tsp. French-style mustard
Red wine vinegar
4 lemons
1 (8-oz.) can medium ripe olives

PREPARATION:
Place cleaned squid in a large skillet with natural juice and ¼ cup olive oil. Sauté over medium heat until squid is barely cooked, turning frequently. Remove, drain well, and let stand. Chop parsley and pimientos. Pour olive oil into a large salad bowl and press half the garlic into the oil. Slice remaining garlic and add to oil. Add anchovies and mash well. Add 2 shakes Worcestershire sauce and mustard. Add red wine vinegar to taste (approximately ¼ cup) and squeeze juice of 2 lemons into mixture. Mix well. Add squid, chopped parsley, pimien-

tos and olives. Toss and refrigerate for at least 5 hours. Mix occasionally. Serve in decorative shallow salad bowl. Garnish with parsley and slices of lemon. Just before serving squeeze 1 or 2 additional lemons on salad.

Makes 10 to 12 servings

Cockles in Garlic Sauce

Though eaten cold with a little vinegar in England and Ireland, Californians like their cockles prepared with—you guessed it—Garlic!

Recipe contest entry: Donald A. Hunter, Novato

35 cockles (or hard-shell clams)
½ yellow onion, sliced in rings
1 cup water
½ cup white wine
4 tbsp. butter
3 cloves fresh garlic, minced
¼ tsp. thyme
½ tsp. minced parsley
1 tbsp. flour, heaping

PREPARATION:
Steam clams with onion rings, water, and white wine until shells open. Remove clam meat and chop well. Reserve 1¼ cups of clam broth. Melt butter and sauté garlic. Add thyme, parsley, and flour. Stir well. Slowly add reserved clam broth and then chopped clams. Simmer for 10 minutes. Serve over noodles or fresh pasta.

Makes 4 servings

Scallops and Mushrooms Brochette

In some areas fresh scallops are becoming difficult to find and small pieces of shark or other fish are being substituted in the marketplace. Our first choice would be scallops, of course, but this recipe could be used with any similar fish. Be sure not to overcook, particularly if using scallops. They should be slightly underdone to be at their best flavor.

2 lbs. fresh scallops
½ cup olive oil
2 tbsp. lemon juice
2 tsp. seasoned salt
½ tsp. garlic salt
¼ tsp. black pepper
1 bay leaf
8 coriander seeds
1 (8-oz.) can mushroom caps, drained

PREPARATION:
Wash and drain scallops and arrange in a flat baking dish. Combine remaining ingredients, except mushrooms, and pour over scallops to coat all sides. Marinate in refrigerator several hours. Preheat broiler. Thread scallops onto skewers alternately with mushroom caps. Place on rack and broil 3 to 4 inches from heat 8 to 10 minutes. Turn and broil 8 to 10 minutes longer. Brush several times with marinade during broiling. Serve with tartar sauce.

Makes 4 to 6 servings

Mixed Seafood Sauté

Seafood lovers will love this seafood combination. It merited an Honorable Mention in the Great Garlic Recipe Contest and Cook-off, and all who tested it rated it excellent, especially when served over rice.

Recipe contest entry: Carmela Meely, Walnut Creek

½ cup butter
2 tbsp. olive oil
½ lb. raw prawns, shells on
½ lb. scallops
½ lb. crab legs, shells on
⅓ cup chopped parsley
6 cloves fresh garlic, minced
3 chopped shallots
2 tbsp. red wine
2 tsp. lemon juice
Salt and pepper to taste
1 tbsp. sherry or Marsala

PREPARATION:
Melt butter in a pan, and add olive oil. Toss in seafood. When prawns turn pink, add parsley, garlic, shallots, white wine, lemon juice, salt and pepper. Heat through. Stir in sherry. Garnish with lemon slices and serve over rice.

Makes 4 servings

Fillets Neapolitan

Although this fish recipe does not contain the cheese usually associated with pizza, it does call for many of the seasonings and the familiar tomato sauce, hence the description, Neapolitan.

¼ cup flour
½ tsp. salt
¼ tsp. black pepper
2 lbs. fish fillets (sole, flounder, perch, etc.)
¼ cup olive oil
1 cup chopped onion
1 (8-oz.) can tomato sauce
1 (6-oz.) can tomato paste
¼ cup water
2 tsp. parsley flakes
½ tsp. sugar
½ tsp. garlic powder
½ tsp. Italian seasoning

PREPARATION:

Combine flour, salt, and pepper. Dredge fish fillets into seasoned flour, then sauté in hot oil until lightly browned on both sides. Remove. Brown onion, then add remaining ingredients. Mix well and simmer 10 minutes. Place fish in sauce and simmer 5 minutes longer or until heated through. Serve with lemon wedges.

Makes 4 to 6 servings

Baked Trout Montbarry

Mrs. Morretti did not share with us the secret of the name "Montbarry." However, we are grateful she has shared her most unusual treatment for trout so that we can pass it along to you.

Courtesy of: Emma Morretti, Gilroy

---

4 tbsp. butter
1 tsp. parsley, finely chopped
1 tsp. onion, finely chopped
4 cloves fresh garlic, minced
3 heaping tsp. finely chopped raw mushrooms
6 trout
Salt and pepper to taste
4 egg yolks
3 tbsp. brandy
5 tbsp. soft breadcrumbs
5 tbsp. grated Parmesan or Romano cheese
Dash of paprika

PREPARATION:

Preheat oven to 400°F. Butter a baking dish thoroughly. Line with mixture of parsley, onion, and garlic. Distribute mushrooms over onion-garlic "crust." Season trout with salt and pepper and place on mushroom layer. Pour over 2 tbsp. melted butter and cover the dish with parchment paper (or brown or waxed), heavily buttered with the remaining 1 tbsp. butter. Bake for 10 minutes. Meanwhile, beat egg yolks well; add brandy. Remove paper from trout and pour egg-brandy mixture over. Sprinkle with breadcrumbs and cheese, then paprika. Serve in its own baking dish.

Makes 6 servings

Tipsy Garlic Shrimp

This sautéed shrimp recipe calls for white wine to make the sauce, and the report is that it makes a delightful contribution to the flavor of the dish.

Recipe contest entry: S. Louise Gershick, Los Angeles

¼ cup butter
3 cloves fresh garlic, crushed
1 cup whole mushrooms, stems removed
1 tbsp. lemon juice
12 oz. fresh shrimp, shelled and deveined
1 cup white wine
2 tbsp. cornstarch mixed with just enough water to dissolve

PREPARATION:

Melt butter in large skilled. Add crushed garlic and whole mushrooms. Gently mix in lemon juice and shrimp. (Add more butter, if needed, at this time.) Sauté 1 minute on each side, or until pink. Add wine; increase heat and bring to a boil. Remove from heat and add cornstarch mixture. Return to flame until sauce is thickened. Serve over rice.

Makes 2 servings

Clams-sailor Style

Although the author of this recipe says the chopped chile is optional, we recommend you include it, because it gives the dish a most distinctive flavor.

Recipe contest entry: Fernandez-Carozzi family, San Mateo

20 medium clams
8 cloves fresh garlic, minced
6 tbsp. olive oil
3 tbsp. chopped fresh parsley
2 tbsp. fine dry breadcrumbs
Salt to taste
1 cup white wine or sherry
1 chile, chopped (optional)

PREPARATION:
Soak clams in salty water for 5 hours before preparing dish, and rinse. In a large pan, sauté garlic in oil. Add parsley and clams; cover 5 to 10 minutes to open the clams. Once clams are open, add breadcrumbs, salt, white wine, and chile. Move pan back and forth for about 5 minutes over medium heat until sauce thickens.

Makes 4 servings

Rice à la Najar

Rice can be the star of the meal when cooked to fluffy perfection with chicken stock, tomato juice, garlic, and other seasonings. Bright green peas and plump pink shrimp add color and eye appeal.

Recipe contest entry: Marina V. Najar, Gardena

2 tbsp. corn oil
2 cups long grain white rice
3 cloves fresh garlic, minced
3 medium green onions, chopped
1 tsp. vinegar
4 cups chicken stock
1 cup sweet peas
½ cup tomato juice
1 tsp. mustard

Salt and pepper to taste
1 tsp. thyme
¼ cup butter or margarine
2 cups cooked shrimp, cleaned
and deveined
Minced parsley for garnish
Paprika for garnish
Pimiento for garnish (optional)

PREPARATION:

Heat oil in a nonstick skillet or pan. Sauté rice (do not brown); add garlic, onions, and vinegar. Stir gently. Add stock, peas, tomato juice, mustard, salt, pepper, and thyme. Stir two or three times gently. Turn heat to medium-high and boil until water reduces to about ½ inch above rice. Lower heat and simmer about 25 to 30 minutes, or until rice is done. Grains should look whole and be easy to separate with a fork. Dot generously with butter or margarine. Top with shrimp and cover, about 10 minutes. Sprinkle with minced parsley and a little paprika and serve piping hot. Tiny pieces of pimiento can also be used, if desired.

Makes 6 to 8 servings

Herb-broiled Salmon Steaks

Custom dictates that the cook be gentle when choosing spices for cooking salmon, lest the fish lose its own distinctive flavor in the process. The seasonings used in this recipe have been carefully selected to blend with and enhance the flavor of the salmon steaks as they broil.

½ cup melted butter
2 tsp. lemon juice
2 tsp. seasoned salt
1 tsp. tarragon
½ tsp. garlic powder
½ tsp. ground marjoram
½ tsp. lemon peel
Dash cayenne or red pepper
2 lbs. salmon steaks

PREPARATION:
Preheat broiler. Combine melted butter and lemon juice with seasonings. Arrange salmon steaks on greased broiler rack and brush with half the seasoned butter. Broil 2 inches from heat for 5 to 10 minutes. Carefully turn and brush with remaining butter mixture. Broil steaks 7 minutes longer or until they flake easily with a fork. Serve hot, garnished with lemon wedges and sprigs of parsley.

Makes 4 servings

Mouthwatering Baked Fish

Jeanne Marks says of her truly mouthwatering baked fish, "The aroma knocks you out." It is good enough to qualify the author as one of the Top Ten finalists who competed in the Great Garlic Recipe Contest and Cook-off.

Recipe contest entry: Jeanne Marks, Aptos

8 to 10 lb. whole fish (salmon, sea bass, red snapper, etc.)
Nonstick vegetable spray
¼ cup brandy or apple juice
½ cup onion flakes
¼ cup oil or melted butter
¼ cup lemon juice
4 cloves fresh garlic, mined or pressed
2 tbsp. Worcestershire sauce
Salt and pepper to taste
Lemon slices
Paprika

PREPARATION:

Rinse and dry fish and place into a baking dish that has been sprayed with nonstick spray. Combine all ingredients and pour over fish. Let stand at least 1 hour. Bake in 400°F-oven for about 30 minutes or until fish flakes and has lost its transparency. Baste at least once during baking process. Decorate top with lemon slices and paprika.

Makes 8 to 10 servings

Baked Codfish Gilroy Style

There are many different kinds of fish, including codfish, available from nearby Monterey Bay and the Pacific Ocean. This recipe, which includes both potatoes and tomatoes, becomes a meal-in-one. Just serve it with a green salad and your favorite wine.

Recipe contest entry: Aurelia Verissimo, Gilroy

⅔ cup vegetable oil
4 cloves fresh garlic, minced
8 sprigs fresh parsley, chopped
6 large new potatoes
2 green onions, chopped
Salt
2 lbs. fresh codfish
1 large tomato
1 lemon
Fresh parsley sprigs

PREPARATION:
Preheat oven to 450°F. Mix oil, garlic, and parsley in a measuring cup. Peel and slice potatoes ¼-inch thick. Mix well with half the garlic mixture and green onions. Spread in a 9 x 13 baking dish. Salt generously. Bake 20 minutes. Remove from oven and place fish fillets on potatoes. Pour remaining garlic mixture evenly over fish. Salt again. Return pan to oven and bake 15 minutes. Garnish with thinly sliced tomatoes, lemon wedges, and parsley.

Makes 6 servings

Trout Cantonese à la Gow

One advantage of Chinese cooking is that it preserves the firm texture of the fish, while the spices selected tend to highlight its flavor, bringing everything into harmony.

Recipe contest entry: Lorraine Soo Storck, Fullerton

2 large trout
1 large bunch scallions or green onions
4 cloves fresh garlic, finely chopped
Fresh ginger root
2 tbsp. soy sauce
4 thinly sliced onion rings
¼ cup bacon drippings
4 large tomatoes
Salt, pepper and garlic powder to taste
1 cup water

PREPARATION:
Preheat oven to 350°F. Clean and slit trout; place in a shallow baking dish. Chop scallions and cover fish. Insert some garlic into slits and sprinkle the remaining garlic on top. Slice ginger into thin strips and lay on fish lengthwise. Sprinkle soy sauce over all. Arrange onion rings in a circle around fish. Pour bacon drippings over all. Quarter tomatoes and place around fish. Season with salt, pepper and garlic, and sprinkle water over all. Cover with aluminum foil and bake for 1 hour at 350°F. Reduce heat to 275°F and bake for another hour. Baste frequently. Serve with steamed rice.

Makes 4 servings

Mock Oyster Stir-fry

An imaginative combination of ingredients transforms this inexpensive, quick dish into a delectable treat. You won't even miss the oysters.

1980 Recipe contest first runner-up: Leonard Brill, San Francisco

½ tbsp. vegetable oil
½ tbsp. sesame oil
3 to 4 cloves fresh garlic, chopped
2 cups sliced zucchini
¼ cup sliced mushrooms
2 cups tofu, cut into ½-inch cubes
1 tbsp. soy sauce
⅓ cup oyster sauce
Sesame seeds

PREPARATION:
Heat oil in a wok or frying pan over medium-high heat. Add garlic, zucchini, and mushrooms. Stir fry until zucchini starts to brown, about 2 minutes. Add tofu and toss. Reduce heat to low-medium. Mix soy sauce and oyster sauce and pour over vegetables and tofu. Toss and cook, covered, 2 to 3 minutes. Remove cover and cook another minute or so until sauce thickens. Sprinkle with sesame seeds.

Serves 4

Scallops Gilroix

An aromatic sauce, thick and bubbling, enfolds tender scallops in this luscious appetizer that's served in individual bowls.

1980 Recipe contest finalist: James Jefferson, Los Gatos

⅓ cup butter
3 large cloves fresh garlic, finely chopped
½ tsp. garlic salt
½ tsp. tarragon, crushed
½ tsp. pepper medley
¼ cup white wine
½ lb. fresh scallops, rinsed and drained
1 tsp. cornstarch
½ cup sour cream

PREPARATION:

Melt butter in a small saucepan. Add garlic, garlic salt, tarragon, pepper medley, and wine. Stir well and bring to a boil. Add scallops and sauté 3 minutes. Thicken the sauce with cornstarch. Reduce heat. When mixture stops boiling, stir in the sour cream. Serve in small bowls. The dish is best as an appetizer. If served as an entrée, double the recipe.

Serves 4

Miscellaneous

There wasn't a thing that couldn't be cured with garlic, according to ancient folklore. From toothaches to colds, to the dangers of vampires, garlic was the protector against all evils. While some of its power is now relegated to superstition, garlic still remains the protector against one dreaded problem—the cooking blahs that can overcome even the best of cooks. Garlic's aromatic flavor perks up the tastebuds, banishing boredom while providing infinite ways to add a lively touch to most dishes. From pickles and relishes, to popcorn and chocolate-covered garlic, these recipes are bound to inspire and get those creative cooking juices flowing again.

Quick and Easy Recipe Ideas

Garlic goes with all dishes, if you give it a chance. Be innovative. Garlic and scrambled eggs? It perks up sluggish morning appetites. Add garlic to soups, salads, and entrées of every kind. And top toast with a garlic spread for a zesty brunch treat.

One recipe contest entrant suggested a flavorful English muffin and garlic treat that is used in her household for colds, flu, or bronchitis: Butter toasted English muffin halves and sprinkle with a minced clove of garlic. Spread with grated cheese, then top with 3 or more cloves of minced garlic. Broil until cheese melts and the garlic is toasted and crispy. Eat with parsley on the side or sprinkle chopped parsley on top of the muffin before eating. Whether or not these garlic muffins give aid to various ailments, their flavor appeal is likely to perk up poor appetites.

Another contest entrant suggests eating garlic with breakfast cereal. She starts with 3 small cloves of fresh garlic and chews them quickly. Then she eats the cereal immediately afterwards. "The cereal removes the sting of the garlic and precludes any smell on your breath," she says. Her reason for eating the garlic is to regulate her blood pressure.

Sabrina's Garlic Soufflé

The youngest entrant in the Garlic Recipe Contest and Cook-off was a teenager whose recipe for garlic soufflé qualified her among the Top Ten finalists. Serve for brunch or as an unusual side dish.

Recipe contest entry: Sabrina Vial, Fresno

¼ cup butter
1 (10½-oz.) can cream of celery soup
½ cup milk
1½ tsp. salt
¼ tsp. pepper
2 cups shredded Cheddar cheese
2 tsp. lemon juice
3 beaten eggs
1 cup minced fresh garlic

PREPARATION:

Preheat oven to 350°F. In a large saucepan, melt butter. Add soup, milk, salt, and pepper; blend over medium heat until smooth. Slowly add cheese and lemon juice, blending well. Remove from heat. Add well-beaten eggs and garlic. Mix well and pour into a greased 1½-quart casserole. Bake uncovered for 50 minutes.

Makes 4 servings

Sunflower Snaps

It's a snap to prepare these sunflower nibbles. They are delicious as a snack and also make a crunchy addition to salads, soups, hot cereal, or baked beans.

Recipe contest entry: Camille Russell, Oakland

1 tbsp. vegetable oil
2 cups raw sunflower seeds, shelled
8 cloves fresh garlic, minced
¼ tsp. salt
1 tbsp. soy sauce

PREPARATION:
Heat oil in a large frying pan over medium-high heat. Add sunflower seeds and garlic. Stir. When a few of the seeds turn golden, reduce heat to medium, and continue stirring as needed. Stop cooking when about half the seeds are golden. Remove from heat and add salt. After 5 minutes add soy sauce and stir. Store in a jar with a tight lid.

Makes 2 cups

Garlic-Basil Popcorn

Popcorn rises to new heights of flavor when tossed with butter, garlic, basil, and Parmesan cheese. Whether for snacking or as party fare, you won't be able to stop eating these crunchy morsels until they're all gone.

Recipe contest entry: S. E. Moray, San Francisco

---

3 extra-large cloves fresh garlic, pressed
2 tbsp. butter or margarine
Pinch of sweet basil
1 tbsp. oil
¼ cup popcorn kernels
Salt to taste
2 tbsp. Parmesan cheese

PREPARATION:

Place garlic in a custard cup, along with butter and sweet basil. Heat a small amount of water in a saucepan and place custard cup in it to melt butter and infuse it with the herbs, or melt in microwave oven 30 seconds. Heat oil in a heavy iron or stainless steel pot. Drop one kernel in the oil, and when it pops, add the rest of the popcorn and cover. Shake pot occasionally as it pops. When all the corn has popped, add butter mixture and stir in vigorously. Add salt and Parmesan cheese and stir or shake to coat well.

Makes 2 servings

Vessey's Deep-fried Garlic

Until you've tried these deep-fried garlic cloves, you probably won't believe how delicious they are or how much fun it is to serve them.

Courtesy of: Wayne Vessey, Hollister

---

2 whole bulbs fresh garlic
Boiling water
1 cup biscuit mix
1 egg
½ cup beer
2 tsp. parsley flakes
½ tsp. salt
Vegetable oil for deep frying

PREPARATION:

Separate bulbs and peel garlic. Drop cloves into boiling water and when boiling resumes, blanch for 3 to 4 minutes. The longer the cloves cook, the milder their flavor, but don't overcook, or they will be mushy. Drain and pour cold water over to cool. Meanwhile, prepare batter by combining biscuit mix, egg, beer, parsley, and salt. Heat vegetable oil in a deep pot or fry cooker. Dip each cooked clove of garlic in batter and fry until golden brown in color. Remove and drain on paper towels. Serve hot.

Makes about 50 to 60 cloves

Garlic-Spiced Walnuts

One of the long-time fruit crops still being produced in Gilroy is walnuts. The addition of a little garlic flavoring, together with ginger and allspice turns them into great between-meal nibbles or cocktail-time snacks.

---

2 tsp. ginger
½ tsp. allspice
5 cups water
1 lb. walnut halves
4 tbsp. melted butter
¾ tsp. garlic salt

PREPARATION:
Preheat oven to 350°F. Add ginger and allspice to water and bring to a boil. Drop in walnuts and boil about 3 minutes. Drain well. Spread in a shallow pan and bake for 15 minutes or until lightly browned. Remove from oven and toss with melted butter and garlic salt.

Makes about 2 cups

Great Garlic Olives

One good reason for the flourishing garlic industry is California's warm climate. In such regions garlic develops its best flavor, and this is probably why it has always been popular in the cuisines that developed in the countries surrounding the Mediterranean.

---

2 (7-oz.) cans pitted ripe olives, drained
3 tbsp. olive oil
2 large cloves fresh garlic, minced
½ tsp. oregano leaves

PREPARATION:

Marinate drained olives in the olive oil, garlic, and oregano in a covered container for a minimum of 4 hours (the longer the better).

Makes about 2 cups

Garlic Relish

Garlic relish adds that extra little touch to dress up simple entrées. With its tomato and eggplant flavor, enhanced with fish paste and garlic, this versatile relish is savory and easy to prepare.

Recipe contest entry: Birgita Muller, Los Angeles

1 large or 2 small eggplants
2 large tomatoes
4 cloves fresh garlic
Salt
1 tsp. fish paste or marmite
1 large onion, thinly sliced
1 tbsp. vegetable oil
1 tsp. brown sugar
2 tsp. chili powder

PREPARATION:
Slice eggplant, sprinkle with salt, and set aside for ½ hour. Cut up tomatoes and remove seeds. Crush garlic and mix with fish paste. Brown onion slightly in oil. Add fish paste, garlic, sugar, and chile powder. Add eggplant and mix all together, blending well. Add tomatoes and cook gently for 5 minutes. Taste and add salt as needed. Transfer mixture into the bowl of a steamer and steam for 20 minutes.

Makes about 3 cups

Garlic Dill Pickles

When cucumbers are plentiful, put up a batch or two of crunchy dill pickles. They're great for sandwiches and to garnish potato, tuna, and other salads.

7 lbs. medium cucumbers
6 thick onion slices
4 tbsp. dill seed
3 tsp. crushed red pepper
¾ tsp. dehydrated garlic
1 quart vinegar
2 quarts water
½ cup salt

PREPARATION:

Wash cucumbers and pack into 6 hot sterilized quart jars. To each jar add 1 slice onion, 2 tsp. dill seed, ½ tsp. crushed red pepper, and ⅛ tsp. garlic. For a stronger flavor, use ¼ tsp. garlic in each jar. Combine remaining ingredients and bring to a boil. Pour, boiling hot, over cucumbers, leaving ¼-inch space at top. Seal at once.

Makes 6 quarts

Paul's Pickled Peppers

If Peter Piper picked a peck of pickled peppers, he'd want to put up a batch with garlic, as in the recipe below.

Courtesy of: Paul Pelliccione, Gilroy

---

7 to 9 large (3 lbs.) green peppers, seeded
Boiling water
2½ cups distilled white vinegar
2½ cups water
1¼ cups granulated sugar
8 cloves fresh garlic, peeled
4 tsp. salad oil
2 tsp. salt

PREPARATION:

Cut peppers lengthwise into ¾-inch strips. Place in a bowl and cover with boiling water. Let stand 5 minutes; drain. Combine vinegar, water, and sugar in a saucepan; boil 5 minutes. Meanwhile pack peppers into 4 hot sterilized pint jars. To each jar add 2 cloves garlic, 1 tsp. salad oil and ½ tsp. salt. Immediately pour in boiling syrup to cover peppers, 1 jar at a time. Fill to within ¼ inch of top. Seal at once.

Makes 4 pints

Garlic Butter

Garlic butters are easy to make and add an extra-special epicurean touch to many dishes. Slather some on bread slices before adding the filling for rich, zesty sandwiches. Brush loaves of French or Italian bread with garlic butter and broil or bake for mouth-watering garlic bread. Use as a spread to perk up simple canapés.

Melt garlic butter over vegetables or grilled meat for incomparable flavor enhancement, or heat some in a skillet to sauté shrimp, lamb, or other meats or vegetables. Use in sauce, to flavor soups, and don't forget escargots—it's not possible to cook these tender morsels without garlic butter!

Make extra garlic butter to keep on hand in the refrigerator (or freezer for longer storage). You'll be surprised at how many new uses you'll discover if you have some readily available.

Hint: Chill garlic butter, roll into logs, cover with plastic wrap and chill until firm. Slice off as needed.

For a novel party idea, gather friends together to make garlic butter. Everyone can take turns peeling garlic cloves and creaming butter. Each guest will have some tasty garlic butter to take home afterwards. What to serve at your garlic party? All sorts of garlic goodies, of course, from appetizers to salads to the entrée, even a garlic dessert if you're daring!

Try one of these combinations for garlic butter.

Basic Garlic Butter

½ cup butter
2 to 3 cloves fresh garlic, pressed or finely minced

PREPARATION:
Cream butter. Add garlic and beat until fluffy.

Makes ½ cup

Garlic Herb Butters

Add freshly chopped chives, shallots, or parsley to basic garlic butter, or select herbs and spices from the spice shelf—Italian herb seasoning, basil, or dill, for example.

Garlic Cheese Butters

Add shredded or grated cheese of your choice to basic garlic butter.

Quickie Garlic Butter

Use ¾ tsp. garlic powder instead of fresh garlic. Add ¼ tsp. salt and a dash black pepper. Let stand for 30 minutes for flavors to blend.

Easy Melt Garlic Butter

Instead of creaming basic garlic butter, just heat butter and garlic over low heat until butter melts. Do not brown!

Extra Garlicky Butter

Mash 6 cloves (or used dehydrated equivalent) of fresh garlic into ½ cup butter.

Delicate Garlic Butter

Blanch and drain 4 cloves of fresh garlic and pound together; combine with ½ cup fresh butter or margarine. Pass the mixture through a fine sieve.

Party Time Garlic Butter

Moisten 1 tsp. of instant granulated garlic with an equal amount of water. Place in a mixer bowl with 1 lb. softened butter or margarine. Beat until very creamy. Let stand about 20 minutes to blend flavors. Butter may also be melted over hot water or in a food warmer and spread with a pastry brush. Makes enough garlic butter for 100 medium pieces of French or Italian bread or 200 slices of bread or bun halves for sandwiches.

Aioli

Probably the most famous garlic sauce of all is aioli, the golden, garlic mayonnaise of Provence. So celebrated is this versatile French sauce that certain days are set aside in many villages for feasts that last from noon until after sundown as platters of vegetables, fish, hard-cooked eggs, and bread are carried in for dipping up the smooth, garlicky delight.

4 large cloves fresh garlic
2 large egg yolks
1 tsp. dry mustard
¼ tsp. salt

¼ tsp. white pepper
1 cup olive oil (use half salad oil,
　if less strong flavor is desired)
1½ tbsp. fresh lemon juice

PREPARATION:
Have all ingredients at room temperature. Combine garlic, egg yolks, mustard, salt, and pepper in a blender jar. Cover and blend at medium speed until smooth. With motor running, remove cover and slowly pour in half the oil in a small steady stream. Stop the motor, and scrape down sides of jar. Cover and turn to medium speed. Uncover and add lemon juice, then remaining oil in a slow stream as before, stopping motor to scrape down sides of jar occasionally as sauce thickens. Chill. Serve with hot or cold fish, cold meat or vegetables.

Makes 1⅓ cups

To prepare sauce with hand or electric mixer: Use a narrow, deep bowl (a 1-quart glass measure makes a good container, or use a smaller bowl supplied with electric mixer). Beat in oil very slowly, especially at the beginning, being sure oil is completely blended before adding more. When thick, crush garlic cloves over sauce and mix well. Chill.

Skordalia

This sauce of fresh garlic has been blended together in the Greek islands since the days of the Argonauts, when, it is said, the searchers for the Golden Fleece passed bowls of *skordalia* around their banquet tables. Sometimes nuts are included. Use ⅓ cup blanched almonds, if you like.

Courtesy of: Katherine Pappas, Gilroy

6 medium potatoes
4 cloves fresh garlic, crushed
2 tsp. salt
1 cup vegetable oil
½ cup white vinegar
3 egg yolks

PREPARATION:

Boil potatoes and put them through masher as for mashed potatoes. Add garlic and salt and let set for 10 minutes. Using a mixer or food processor, mix potatoes and garlic, slowly adding the oil and vinegar, alternating each. (You may add more vinegar if you like a more tart flavor.) After ingredients are thoroughly mixed, add the egg yolks to make the mixture fluffy. Delicious on bread, crackers, and fresh vegetable.

Makes about 1 quart

Garlic Barbecue Dressing

A good and garlicky barbecue sauce with any kind of meat.

Recipe contest entry: Mirta Richards, Cerritos

2 cups hot water
⅔ cup vinegar
½ cup oil
15 whole peppercorns
10 cloves fresh garlic, crushed
4 bay leaves, crushed
1½ tbsp. oregano
1 tbsp. parsley
1 tbsp. salt
1 tsp. rosemary

PREPARATION:

Mix all ingredients in a jar with a tight-fitting lid and shake well. Refrigerate overnight or longer—the longer the better. Baste meat several times while cooking.

Makes about 1 pint

Leo's Garlic Barbecue Sauce

A zesty sauce for the backyard barbecue or the gourmet kitchen.

Courtesy of: Leo Goforth, Gilroy

¾ cup vegetable oil
¾ cup olive oil
5 cloves fresh garlic, pressed
4 sprigs fresh rosemary
2 tbsp. wine vinegar
1 tsp. oregano
1 tsp. salt
1 tsp. black pepper
1 tsp. Tabasco sauce
1 tsp. Worcestershire sauce

PREPARATION:

Blend all ingredients 1 hour before using. For chicken and ribs, add 4 tbsp. catsup.

Makes about 1¾ cups

Louie's Special Marinade

If you're lucky enough to have some fresh game, you'll want to marinate it using this special recipe. This marinade may be used two to three times. How much or how little you should prepare depends on the amount of meat, so let your experience be your guide.

Courtesy of: Louis Bonesio, Jr., Gilroy

---

2 cups dry wine
2 cups vinegar
½ cup catsup
2 medium onions, quartered and sliced
8 to 10 whole cloves
8 to 10 drops Tabasco sauce

4 cloves fresh garlic, crushed
3 bay leaves
2 tsp. coarse black pepper
½ tsp. thyme
½ tsp. dry mustard
½ tsp. oregano

PREPARATION:

Combine all ingredients until well-blended. Do *not* use a metal container for the marinade, but crockery, glass, or plastic. It is advisable to turn the meat occasionally in the marinade.

The marinade may be used for venison and other antlered game, such as elk and antelope, as well as for domestic meats, such as beef and lamb. Usually 24 hours is more than enough for the meat to marinate. If you prefer the gamey flavor, then shorten the time. Since the gamey taste in venison is carried in the fat, it should be removed prior to cooking. The lean meat should be cooked with a small amount of pork fat, butter, or oil to replace the natural fat that has been removed.

Makes about 1 quart

Sicilian Gems

Chocolate-coated garlic cloves? Why not! The recipe's originator says, "Garlic is very good for you. Particularly for high blood pressure. These little Sicilian gems are a wonderful way to get your family to eat garlic and enjoy it!"

Recipe contest entry: Margaret Buccery, Palos Verdes

3 large garlic bulbs (about 30 cloves)
Ice water
½ lb. sweet dark chocolate
1 tbsp. Grand Marnier or liqueur of you choice
Ground walnuts (optional)

PREPARATION:

Separate and peel cloves of garlic. Soak in ice water to seal in flavor and juices while you are preparing the chocolate. Melt chocolate in a double-boiler or fondue pot; add liqueur and blend well. Dry garlic cloves and dip until completely covered in the chocolate/liqueur mixture. Allow to harden, and serve on a small elegant dish at the end of the meal, with cappuccino. These are the *piece de resistance* at the finale of a long and sumptuous Italian meal! (They may also be rolled in ground nuts before they harden, but they are just as good plain.)

Makes about 30 candies

Garlic Pudding

During the Garlic Festival, Digger Dan's, a Gilroy restaurant, featured this unusual dessert on their menu. Although the recipe calls for quite a lot of garlic, it is surprisingly light and flavorful.

2 bulbs fresh garlic
1½ cups cold water
1 cup sugar
1 envelope unflavored gelatin
¼ cup lemon juice
1 tsp. lemon peel, grated
2 egg whites
¼ tsp. mustard
Custard Sauce
¼ tsp. salt
¼ cup lemon juice

PREPARATION:
Wrap garlic bulbs in foil and bake until done (soft). Remove from foil and boil in water until flavor is transferred from bulbs to water and water is reduced to about 1¼ cups. In a saucepan combine sugar, gelatin and salt. Add ½ cup garlic water; stir until dissolved and remove from heat. Add remaining ¾ cup garlic water, lemon juice, and lemon peel. Chill until partially set. Turn into a large bowl. Add egg whites and beat with electric mixer until mixture begins to hold its shape. Turn into mold. Chill until firm. Unmold and garnish with sprinkled nutmeg and custard sauce.

Custard Sauce

4 egg yolks, beaten
¼ cup sugar
2 cups mill
Dash salt

PREPARATION:

In a heavy saucepan, mix egg yolks with sugar, milk, and salt. Cook over low heat until mixture coats a spoon. Cool and serve.

Makes 4 servings

Garlic-laced specialties were prepared in gigantic pans from morning to night as wave after wave of festival goers followed their noses to the bustling outdoor kitchen area.

Vacaville Reporter

Garlic Glossary

Bulb. The name for the usable portion of fresh garlic made up of as many as 15 or more individual cloves.

Clove. One of the several segments of a bulb, each of which is covered in a thin, papery skin.

Crushed. Refers to fresh garlic that has been smashed by the broad side of a knife or cleaver on a chopping board, or with a rolling pin between several thicknesses of waxed paper.

Dehydrated. Any of several forms of garlic from which the moisture has been removed. Dehydrated garlic is available minced, powdered, and granulated.

Fresh. The term used to describe garlic which has not been dehydrated. Actually "fresh" garlic is allowed to "cure" in the field before harvesting just until the paper skin, not the clove, becomes dry.

Garlic Braid. A garland of fresh garlic braided together by its tops. Braiding is done while the garlic is still only partially cured with some moisture remaining in the tops and before the tops are removed in harvesting. When the tops become fully dried, they are too brittle to braid. Originally devised as a convenient storage method that was used around the world, garlic braids are quite decorative and have become popular in this country as a kitchen adornment. Serious garlic lovers like to use them for cooking purposes, cutting off one bulb at a time from the braid. Care should be taken if the braid is to be preserved as a decoration that it is not handled carelessly. The papery covering on the bulbs is fragile and will break easily when the garlic itself has shriveled after a year or so.

Granulated. A dehydrated form of garlic that is five times stronger than raw garlic. Its flavor is released only in the presence of moisture.

Juice. Garlic juice may be purchased commercially or prepared by squeezing fresh cloves in a garlic press, being careful not to include any of the flesh. Juice blends easily for uniform flavor.

Minced. This term is used for both dehydrated and fresh garlic. Generally called for when small pieces of garlic are desirable as in soups, sauces, or salad dressings. Fresh garlic may be minced using a sharp knife on

Garlic Glossary

a chopping board. If the recipe calls for salt, add it while mincing to prevent the garlic from sticking to the knife. It will also absorb the juices otherwise lost in the mincing process. Finely minced garlic, as called for in most French recipes, tends to disappear into the finished dish. For a more robust flavor, mince more coarsely as called for in many Chinese dishes. Large amounts of garlic can be minced using a blender or food processor.

Powdered. Powdered garlic is available commercially. When using powder in recipes with a high acid content, mix with water (2 parts water to 1 part powder) before adding. Powdered garlic can be made from fresh by slowly drying peeled garlic cloves in the oven. When very dry, pound or crush until fine and powdery. Pass through a sieve and pound any large pieces, then sieve again. Store in sealed jars in a dry place.

Pressed. A term for garlic that has been put through a garlic press. There are many different types of presses available, and some that are self-cleaning. When using a garlic press, it isn't necessary to peel the garlic clove. Simply cut it in half and place in the press. Then squeeze. The skin will stay behind, making the press easier to clean. Remember to clean your press immediately after use before the small particles which remain have a chance to dry.

Purée. A term for garlic that has been cooked at high heat and then pressed through a sieve. Available commercially or made at home, it is excellent to have on hand to blend into soups, sauces, or to spread on slices of bread to serve with hors d'oeuvres.

Garlic salt. Available commercially. It is usually a blend of approximately 90% salt, approximately 9%, garlic and approximately 1% free-flowing agent. When using garlic salt in recipes calling for fresh garlic, decrease the amount of salt called for.

Cooking Equivalents Table

Kitchen Measure

3 teaspoons = 1 tablespoon
2 tablespoons = 1 fluid ounce
16 tablespoons = 1 cup
8 ounces = 1 cup or ½ pound
16 ounces = 1 pound
2 cups = 1 pint
2 pints = 1 quart
4 pints = 2 quarts or ½ gallon
4 quarts = 1 gallon

Metric Measure

1 ounce = 28.35 grams
1 gram = 0.35 ounce
8 ounces = 226.78 grams or ½ pound
100 ounces = 3½ ounces
500 grams = 1 pound (generous)
1 pound = ½ kilogram (scant)
1 kilogram = 2¼ pounds (scant)
⅒ liter = ½ cup (scant) or ¼ pint (scant)
½ liter = 2 cups (generous) or 1 pint (generous)
1 quart = 1 liter (scant, or .9463 liter)
1 liter = 1 quart (generous, or 1.0567 quarts)
1 liter = 4½ cups or 1 quart 2 ounces
1 gallon = 3.785 liters (approximately 3¾ liters)

Index

Index

Index

Index

Index

Index

Index